Reviews

Ricci has had significant experience as both a vocal performer and educator. *I Can Sing, But Where is My Voice?* is a clear reflection of this. Not only does this book contain a wide range of very practical, measurable exercises and strategies to help the student to improve the quality of their singing but it also addresses the singer as a whole person.

The voice is a unique instrument in that it exists within the body of the performer. Ricci is obviously acutely aware of this and has explored many ways of improving a person's well-being which then has a positive impact on their ability to realise their potential as a vocalist.

I am confident that this thought-provoking book will be a valuable resource for singers regardless of their level of experience.

Phil Hornblow, B.Mus, A.MusT.C.L,
Vision Studios, Wellington New Zealand

'Passion' and 'hard work' come to mind when reading *I Can Sing, But Where is My Voice?* Ricci has voiced (sic) her thoughts, knowledge and practical experience in an informative way, not only on singing and the voice, but on a number of issues associated with voice projection and what is expected of a quality vocalist. There is plenty of useful information in this book for every aspiring singer.

Gavin Hawley, Composer/Arranger/Musician,
Queensland

The book *I Can Sing, But Where is My Voice?* is a very well thought out and written guide for those who, for enjoyment or a future in singing, can use as a practical guide in every aspect. There is plenty of information; advice (as what to expect, health, posture and much more). How to begin and what is necessary. The instructions are very clear and easy to follow. Included are student's comments which were a good insight to the success that was achieved for each one. The career photo gallery was an interesting aspect, for this helped me to know the teacher and of the achievements attained. This in turn I found encouraging. It's a delightful book with much to offer for many a person's achievement in the excellence of singing.

Diane Corser, Cert III in Education Support,
Logan Qld

This is an amazing guide on how to become a confident singer as well as a happy person. In this book are many helpful, encouraging tips giving choices for singers such as alcohol, drugs and cigarettes, tattoos and how each one can affect the singing voice. There are some interesting student's stories in her book where they advise what positive things happened for their own voices.

Simona Smaidziunaite Korkus, B.A Lithuanian
University of Educational Sciences, Child Educator.

Have you always wanted to become a singer? Ricci Carr has developed a foolproof method to help you realise your dreams. She knows her subject very well, having come from a professional voice background. If you follow Ricci's program, you will certainly improve your singing range, accuracy and stamina. It's a practical, easy to follow book that every singer should read!

Judy Newman,
Gold Coast Queensland

What a marvellous book it is — concise, covers everything and very positive. It ought to sell well to aspiring performers.

Peter Blake, Ear, nose and throat specialist, particular interest in treating professional artists, including announcers and singers.

I Can Sing!

But Where is My Voice?

A MODERN SINGER'S GUIDE

Ricci Carr

Published in Australia by Silverbird Publishing
luke@workingtype.com.au
First published in Australia 2015
This edition published 2019
Copyright © Ricci Carr 2016
Cover design, typesetting: WorkingType (www.workingtype.com.au)

Editor (1st edn): Spiegel, Angela
Publication management and design for 2nd Edition: Luke Harris
The right of Ricci Carr to be identified as the Author of the Work has been asserted in accordance with the Copyright, Designs and Patents Act 1988.

The Author of this book accepts all responsibility for the contents and absolves any other person or persons involved in its production from any responsibility or liability where the contents are concerned.

All rights reserved. No part of this publication may be reproduced, stored in a retrieval system, or transmitted, in any form or by any means without the prior written permission of the publisher, nor be otherwise circulated in any form of binding or cover other than that in which it is published and without a similar condition being imposed on the subsequent purchaser.

I Can Sing, But Where is My Voice?
Author: Ricci Carr
All rights reserved. No part of this publication may be reproduced, stored in a retrieval system, or transmitted in any form or by any means, electronic, mechanical, photocopying, recording or otherwise, without the prior written permission of the author.

National Library of Australia Cataloguing-in-Publication entry

Author:	Carr, Ricci
Editor (2nd edn)	Luke Harris
Title:	I Can Sing, But Where is My Voice?
	by Ricci Carr
ISBN:	978-0-6485893-5-8 (paperback)
Subjects:	Singing--Diction
	Voice culture
	Singing--Studies and exercises
	Popular music
Dewey No:	783.043

SCIS record no: 1768819 FOR I CAN SING BUT WHERE IS MY VOICE?

SCIS record no:	1768819
ISBN:	978-0-6485893-5-8
Title:	I can sing but where is my voice? : a modern singer's guide / Ricci Carr.
Main author:	Carr, Ricci.
Publisher:	Silverbird Publishing, PO Box 72, Eltham VIC 3095
Description:	iii, 132 pages : illustrations (some colour), music, portraits.
Subjects:	Singing - Study and teaching.
	Singing - Problems, exercises, etc.
	Voice - Care and health.
	Popular music.
Call nos:	783 CAR (abridged Dewey)
	783.043 CAR (Full Dewey)
Notes:	Summary: Wondering how you can get to sing that song you always wanted to without running out of breath, and sing it all in tune? Need to sing at your best friend's wedding or maybe in a school production? Perhaps you want to sing with a band. Start a professional career or maybe you are a grandparent who just wants to know that every time you sing to your grandchildren you are singing those family songs in tune. With this book finally there is a guide for the student who wants to know how to sing well. This guide will help you to identify what it is you need to know and gives you the tools to apply the skills required. Advice that works given time and genuine input from you, the singer. (From back cover).

*I dedicate this work to
my grandson Jack,
whom I love dearly.
Always on my mind.*

Introduction

Being an actor and a singer I am always conscious of my voice. I use it every day. At the moment I am touring Australia and performing in a different theatre every week. As they say: "The show must go on," so I need to make sure my voice is as fit as it can be when the curtain rises. Reading through *I can sing, but where is my voice?* has reminded me of some basic steps that are vital to keep your voice working at its best when you need it the most. The section of the book that I can relate to most is 'Correcting faults'. In the past few months my singing range has grown simply by correcting my posture, relaxing my jaw and resonating my high notes through the hard palate of my mouth. It is good to see there is now a book out there that is easily understood by beginners and a good reminder for professionals.

Tom Oliver *is one of Australia's brightest rising talents with a broad portfolio that includes music, theatre, film, television and cabaret. In 2014, Tom became a member of Kylie Minogue's inaugural team on Channel 9's hit television show* The Voice Australia.

Table of Contents

Introduction 5
Realising your singing dreams 8
Know the basics 9
Assessment 12
Correcting faults 15
High resonance diagram 23
Low resonance diagram 24
Getting Started 30
Practice – breathing exercises and charts – the daily grind 33
Using a glottal stroke 38
Vowel pronunciation 39
Sounds to practice 40
Physical warm-ups 44
How to practice (beginners, intermediate
and well developed students) 46
Choosing which songs suit your voice 49

Performance on the day	52
Microphone technique	55
Frequently asked questions	57
Question time	63
Students' stories	67
Your health as a singer	79
The voice, the popular song and the singer	80
Complementary medicine (naturopathy and herbal medicine)	87
Long-term health choices for singers	91
Scales and sounds to practice	95
Worksheets	100
Answers to question time	104
Photo gallery (1960s, 1970s, 1980s, 1990s and early 2000s)	110
Acknowledgements	131
Where can I buy an eBook?	132

Introduction

My experience comes from more than 45 years as a singer, songwriter and vocal coach. I have sung and performed live in many countries including Australia, Noumea, Tonga, Fiji, Vietnam, Japan, East Asia, New Zealand, the USA, and Denmark. I have taught many students – novices and more seasoned performers. My book *I can sing, but where is my voice?* is the culmination of my experience and knowledge gleaned along the way. In it I share with you the practical techniques, skills and knowledge that worked for me to help you develop your singing ability. With the right attitude, persistence and hard work, you can have the joy and satisfaction that comes from realising your dream to sing and sing well.

I can sing, but where is my voice? is a holistic approach to singing and incorporates the basic skills to develop your voice. It includes some inspiring stories from students to encourage you, and advice from complementary health professionals on how to keep your body and voice healthy.

After students have done the work and learned the techniques, I have seen them gain the confidence and courage to go out and use their voices to their maximum potential for their own pleasure and to share their gift with others. This has convinced me that the reason teachers are here is to unleash this ability in their students.

Finding the teacher who can help you with this and allows you to be yourself is half the battle. Along the road you may encounter several teachers. Each will give you a different perspective and introduce different methods. This will help you grow. It is important that you are comfortable and able to communicate with your teacher, who should be supportive and non-judgmental in their approach. You may experience several teachers before you find one with these qualities.

The time it takes to learn to sing may vary for different people, but anyone who is determined and can hear sounds can succeed. Whether you are a child who wants to impress your friends at a school concert, an adult who wants to sing in a band, or a grandparent who wishes to sit a grandchild on your knee and sing in tune – improving your voice is possible.

This book aims to give the basic skills required to sing a modern song. Here you will find a simple step-by-step approach that will teach you the basics of singing and inspire you to pursue your singing dreams. There is also a review sheet that you can copy and use to regularly check your progress. You will get results by regular practice and persistence. Singing is great fun. What you need to do now is get started.

GOLD ARTIST AWARD

RADIOINDY.COM

RadioIndy.com has named you a Gold Artist

Dear Ricci Carr,

We screen thousands of songs by indie artists and name the best artists RadioIndy.com Gold Artists. We focus on musicianship, songwriting and recording quality when determining your Gold artist status. Congratulations - You are a Radioindy Gold Artist! Feel free to copy/paste the Gold Artist Logo above onto any website(s) to announce your award.

If there is ever anything we can do to improve your experience on RadioIndy.com, please let us know.

Congratulations,

Manny and Greg
Co-Founders, RadioIndy.com

MikVacch Enterprises, LLC (Radioindy.com)

support@radioindy.com • RadioIndy.com

June 2007

Realising Your Singing Dreams

Success in music is roughly 25 per cent natural ability and 75 per cent hard work.

Learning to sing is a lot of work, but it can also be incredibly rewarding. What it takes is determination, a dream, and a good deal of inner strength. This may spring from faith, race, or upbringing. This inner strength will pull you through the worst nightmares of your life and help you to cope and move on. Believe in yourself, for as surely as you were born, you have the right to "be".

You can realise your dreams, but remember, everyone has to chop wood and carry water (i.e. you have to do the work). If you do not, disappointment is a sure thing. Often, people with lesser ability surpass people with more ability because they have a plan. They have a dream that they learn to apply through steady input, which arises from their own heart's desire.

Desire is a powerful thing to have because it allows you to continue to strive for your dreams regardless of what comments other people may make, teachers included. Every individual will make it in their own time. No two people will be the same. In order to succeed, the dream and desire must be your own and not someone else's. You should do this because you want to. Not because someone else wants you to.

Know the Basics

Below is a list of some of the basics that any beginning singer will need to practice on a regular basis.

1. Deep breathing for singing, i.e. deep diaphragmatic breathing.

2. Scales and exercises (both physical and vocal) to gradually strengthen your voice and develop your ear for the correct pitch of notes.

3. Mastering long, smooth notes.

4. Good diction and acquiring the international vowel sounds. Practice in front of the mirror. This involves making letters sound agreeable and depends on where your jaw, tongue, and lips are placed for a given sound. This placement shapes what you sound like to others who listen to you. You should strive to make the vowels sound perfect, i.e. A-E-I-O-U. Nothing else is acceptable for singing.

5. How to apply the correct high and low resonance.

6. To be still inside.

All good performers will have acquired these skills. Just like in everyday speech, lazy vowels, breath before tone (air released before sound) and running words together is unacceptable. If you do not acquire good techniques, as time passes, the audience, whether one or many, will tell you it is unacceptable in no uncertain terms.

The hard work put into practicing breathing, scales, and diction will give you the positive results you want of personal satisfaction, applause, and favourable comments from your audience. It is worth striving for. So give yourself a set time each day to practice and stick to it.

Finally, if for any given time you could practice every working day for six to eight hours, within six months you would have the basic breathing technique perfected for life. However, we all have either work to go to, school, exams to prepare for, rent to pay, cars to run, food to buy, cooking meals, washing, ironing, sickness, job changes, holidays, friendships to nurture and leave time for some fun. This does not leave much time for singing practice. But if you really want to grasp the concept of singing, and you find time in the first 12 months to practice regularly, you will be pleased with your results.

Know that it is not always the singer with the loudest voice who wins. It is the intelligent singer who knows how to apply the basic techniques that wins in the end.

Assessment

Picture this. You want to sing at your best friend's wedding in 10 months' time and you have made the move to finally go ahead and take that first lesson. You make a few enquiries with music shops and search for music teachers on the internet and the yellow pages. One of them stands out and you go for it, not quite knowing what to expect, but you try to keep an open mind. You make a call and find out you need to prepare two songs to sing on the day. When you arrive, your nerves begin to get the better of you, but the greeting at the door puts you at ease and helps you keep your composure. After filling out a few relevant details, it is time to sing your two songs for assessment. An assessment could equally apply for those of you who wish to sing for any other reason.

You are given the choice to sing without accompaniment, with a backing track, or while playing your own musical instrument. Once you have finished your songs, the teacher plays some scales and you are asked to repeat certain sounds, singing some notes. It is all new ground, but you push on, singing a long note and performing various other exercises for the voice.

Your teacher is supportive. There are things you certainly need to improve, but there is hope for you yet. After all, there are only a few bad habits any singer ever has and they can be rectified given time and attention to detail.

You will find an assessment is worthwhile because it helps you identify what to work on to improve your singing.

On assessment, you might find that you:

1. Breathe in through your nose at times and you raise your shoulders when taking a breath.

2. Take too many breaths in a given phrase.

3. Use a lot of breath before tone. Air escapes before the sound does.

4. Sing some notes out of tune.

5. Sing some notes out of time.

6. You run out of breath, and are unable to hold a long note steadily

7. Frequently run words together so they are unclear to the listener's ear.

8. Your high notes sound wobbly and thin, so you might be raising your head.

9. Your posture is incorrect. You seem to stand awkwardly with feet together, wearing high heeled shoes, or on one leg with your head to one side.

10. You close your eyes.

11. In part of your song, you seem to be singing high one second, but cannot reach the low notes the next. Your voice gets tired and cracks.

Whatever should be done? You have never had to think about these sorts of things before but, as you would really like to sing at the wedding, you decide maybe you will give some more lessons a go.

There is no human being who cannot be taught to sing unless they cannot hear. All of your problems can be fixed with a little information and encouragement. The length of time it takes is entirely up to you. In this instance, it is a good idea to give yourself six to ten months to correct them.

Correcting Faults

If you want to achieve good results in the end, brace yourself and decide what you want to learn.

Below is a breakdown of some common faults and how to correct them.

Breathing through the nose

Breathing through the nose is something that all singers need to avoid. It causes high notes to be incorrectly executed from the throat or through the nose. This often results in a singer taking shallow breaths that cause them to run out of breath quickly. Instead, singers must learn to breathe through the mouth, to and from the diaphragm, keeping the shoulders still. The best way to learn this is by doing breathing exercises on a daily basis to build up the power of your singing voice and master the techniques you will need to use if you want to sing a song to the best of your potential.

Taking too many breaths that are noisy or short

Breathing for singing is the exact opposite of the sub-conscious breathing you are familiar with in everyday life. Instead of breathing in and out through the nose, the singer must breathe in and out through the mouth, to and from the diaphragm.

If you take too many breaths that are noisy or short, you need to improve your breathing technique. To gain control, regularly practice deep diaphragmatic breathing. There are two exercises that you should practice on a daily basis on pages 35 and 37. Make sure you are relaxed, have a clean quiet space to practice in, and a stopwatch to record your progress.

Breath before tone

Breath before tone simply makes a weak sound instead of a strong one. This means air escapes before the sound and what can be heard is another sound in front of the one you are trying to make (e.g. "i" sounding like "hi"). This can be corrected by applying some form of glottal attack or stroke. A glottal stroke is when both air and sound are released at the same time, giving a clean sound. It involves closing the vocal chords firmly (making an "i" as in "it" sound) before releasing a vowel sound, while at the same time applying the correct position of the jaw and mouth. When applied to words that start with a vowel, this results in a crisp, clear sound. This is what the audience wants to hear so they can enjoy what you are singing. On pages 40–43 in 'Sounds to practice', there are exercises that can help you achieve a crisp, clear sound.

Singing out of tune

Firstly, check to make sure that whatever instrument you are working with is in tune (that is, at A440 standard concert pitch). It is very important to have a tuning instrument or tuning fork handy. A tuning fork looks like a two pronged fork that, when struck against something solid, will give you the correct pitch. Electric pianos and synthesisers have tuners automatically built into them. Some are adjustable, and some are fixed. Electric grand pianos are factory pre-set to standard pitch and should not need to be tuned. Ensuring your instrument is tuned will save a lot of stress when things are not working out for you. By this I mean that you have practiced and practiced at home, but when you have sung the song with others at a rehearsal, it sounded dreadful. It may well be that it was the instrument that was out of tune, rather than your voice! Another common problem for singers is that the song itself may be in the wrong key for your voice. The keys that suit males and females often vary. This may explain why you are singing low one moment and high the next and the song could be in the wrong key for you. Sing your song to the musician you are working with and let them indicate your preference. Write it down so you have a record for future when you sing that particular song again. Not every song will be in the same key for you. This may explain why you are singing low one moment and high the next and the song could be in the wrong key for you.

The next thing to do if you are singing out of tune is learn to listen to yourself. You must be able to hear your mistakes and correct them if you wish to improve. How often have you listened to all 37 notes of a three octave range? All notes need to be listened to and repeated gently at first. Soft singing is far better than belting out unwisely. One loud shout can damage vocal chords permanently. It is important to make sure you execute each vowel sound with some form of a glottal stroke (i.e. soft or strong) for clarity.

Gradual practice will build this clarity up over a period of time, but it will be at least six months before you are able to stand and sing with confidence. Learning to sing is like building the foundations of a house. First, the land is cleared and the foundations put in, then the walls and roof and so on, until it is finished. If it is all done properly, the results are pleasing. It is exactly the same way with singing. Slowly build the foundations – the basics of breathing, scales, exercises, and diction – then you will have what you want in the long term.

The third area to look at when you are singing out of tune is how your breath is coming out with the words you sing. Is it too fast? In spurts? Wobbly? Is it being forced? To make a good sound, the breath must come from the diaphragm and must not be forced. It is necessary to make sure you are using your mouth when you take a breath, rather than your nose. A good test to ensure air is not coming out too fast when you are singing is to place the palm of your hand five centimetres from your mouth as you sing a phrase. You want to make sure almost no air is being released, only the tiniest breath as you execute your phrase. This way, if you have to take a one or half beat rest, you can hold the breath without taking another, thus enabling yourself to finish the phrase with emotion, the way the audience would like to hear it.

The final thing to address on the singing out of tune subject is that your high resonance has to be working for you. High resonance is simply using the correct spaces of the head to execute high sounds. When the air and the sound are placed on the hard palate (roof of the mouth) whilst humming, you should experience a slight vibration either side of the nose, high on the cheek bones. If you feel this vibration whilst singing a note, then your resonance is correct. Be aware that high notes must not be sung from the throat or through the nose because this changes the sound entirely and can damage the vocal chords. Good singing is about being able to control the air coming out. An accomplished teacher will guide you through this area.

In the next section, work on scales and exercises that help you hear the pitch of notes. Follow the scales and exercises from the books of Roland Foster, Dame Nellie Melba or similar, and then try singing with an instrument that is tuned to A440 standard concert pitch.

Timing

It is important to listen to how many beats are being played before you start singing your song. When you know how many beats to wait for, count them and then attack the first note. Do not come in after the beat or in the middle of a word. If you do, you will lose your audience before you begin. An audience is there to hear every word you have to sing, so it is up to you to make it interesting.

In most modern songs, there is an instrumental introduction. It can be two bars of 4/4, four bars of 4/4, eight bars of 4/4, 16 bars of 4/4 and so on. All this means is that there are four beats in a bar. If you have a two bar introduction when the instruments start, you count from the very first beat as one to four, two times, and come in somewhere in the next bar depending on where the beat is that you are required to sing on.

The same will apply for any other timing set by the composer. It could be 2/4, 3/4, or 6/8 for instance. Remember that when you finish your song, you must hold the proper number of beats on your last note (i.e. you cannot run out of breath). There is nothing worse than coming to the end of your song and running out of breath. As far as the audience is concerned, you have lost it. You will be hard pressed to get any applause from such a finish.

You run out of breath, and are unable to hold a long note steadily

If you do not have the breath to hold a long steady note, the solution is to indulge in regular deep diaphragmatic breathing and long note practice. Well executed long notes can bring an audience to you and make you feel really good about your performance.

It is worth spending the better part of a year to familiarise yourself with them.

But what are long notes and how do I practice them?

Long notes are beautifully held suspended sounds that are generally placed at the end of a song. In musical terms, a long note is measured in beats. It may be as short as four beats or as long as 32 beats. To hold such a note with composure, feeling, correct resonance, and smooth delivery will bring an exceptional reaction from any audience. They will want more.

Frequently running words together

In singing, nothing less than perfect pronunciation is acceptable. If the audience cannot understand what it is you are singing, the message and beauty of your song will often be lost. An example of poor execution would be singing the words "won't you" as "won't chew" or "won' you". In an instance such as this, you need to be sure where the emphasis lies in both words. Is it a short sound or a long sound? Hard or soft? In this case, the letter "t" needs to be heard as a subtle sound, but the main emphasis is on the "won".

Often the sound you will have trouble with will be a vowel sound and it will take you a lot longer to perfect than the others. It happened to me, but I persisted and I am really pleased that I did. For me, it was "a" and it took me three months before I conquered that relaxed sound of singing the single "a" in scales. I just could not keep my mouth open for the whole length of my scales or get my tongue to lie flat as my jaw got tired. Instead, I produced a dull sound that was not interesting to the listener's ear. When I finally realised the solution was keeping my mouth open longer, it made a tremendous difference. To this day, I still get people coming up to me and saying things like: "I was at the back of the room and I heard every word you sang". Comments like these make a singer toil for excellence and make you feel good inside.

To sing high notes

1. Stand in front of a mirror armed with a stopwatch to time yourself and a chart to record your progress.

2. Take a deep breath through the mouth, directing the air to the roof of the mouth.

3. Choose a vowel sound and sing it using the correct position of the mouth and employing a glottal stroke. Continue with this exercise through all the vowel sounds.

4. Pick any note that is comfortable and execute it smoothly (no vibrato or wobble).

5. Sing it for as long as possible until your breath runs out.

6. Write down the honest result of your efforts and watch your confidence grow as you continue to practice and record your results on a regular basis.

Good results are achieved when you can sing your long note for 25 seconds or longer. Allow six to twelve months for best results.

High notes sound wobbly and thin; you may be raising your head

This is a sign you are breathing incorrectly. It is generally caused by one of two mistakes:

1. You may have taken a breath through the nose or a shallow breath through the mouth and forced the air out at throat level, forgetting to use head resonance. Head resonance refers to the placement of the sound in the correct space in the head. Sometimes inexperienced singers will place high notes in the throat (this restricts the sound) or through the nasal cavities (which will sound thin and reedy). However, the correct and easiest space to place them is in the roof of the mouth, the hard palate. The easiest way to overcome breathing through the nose or forcing the air out at throat level, is to breathe from the diaphragm to bypass the throat when delivering sound. This ensures the resonance of the head or chest (for low notes) is correct. Resonance refers to the defining of the sound emitted from the vocal chords by the cavities above the throat (larynx).

High Resonance

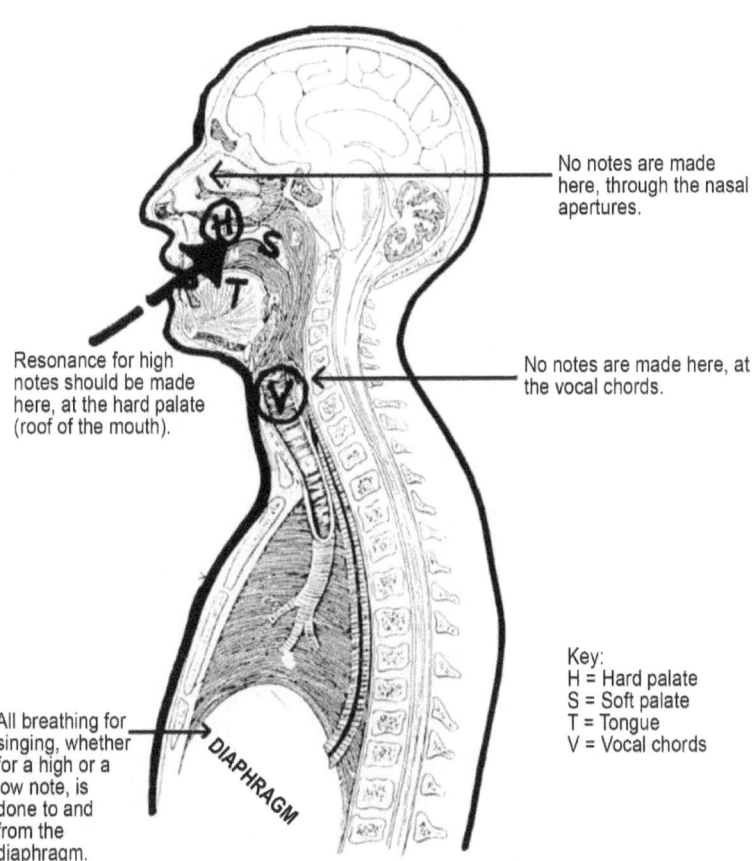

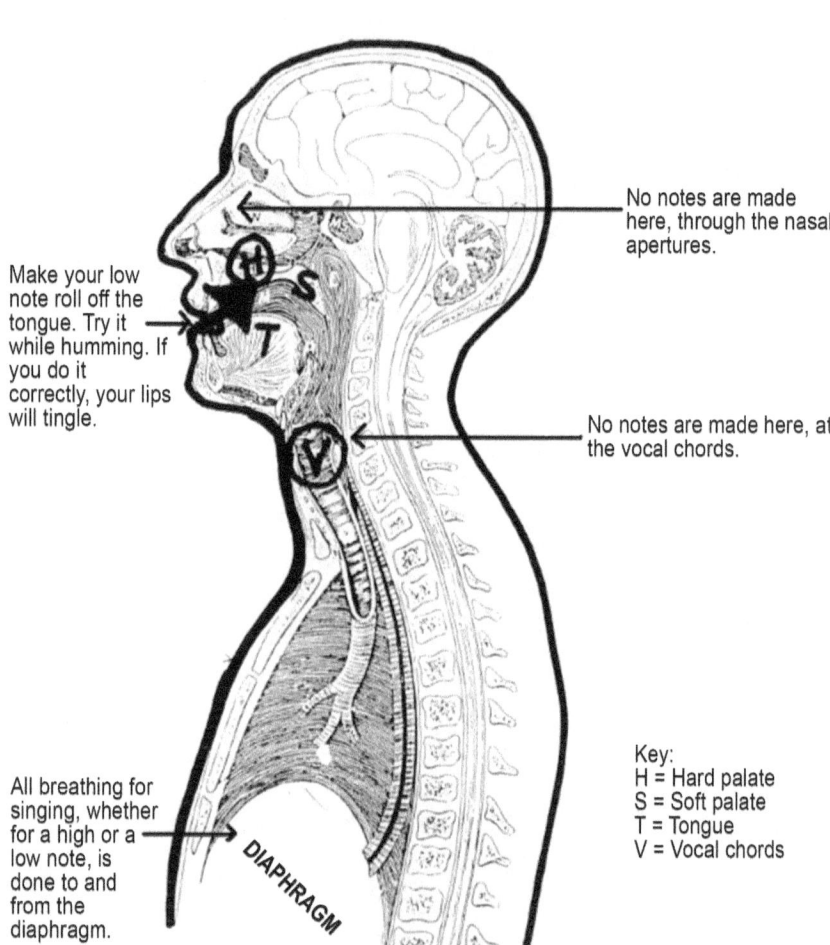

2. Another common mistake is raising your head in an effort to achieve those higher notes. This tightens all the muscles that support the larynx and forces the vocal chords out of sync. Raising your head while singing a high note often causes you to make a thin, tight sound, rather than the concentrated clear sound you desire. You must always try to keep your head level and reach your targeted notes by using the correct resonance.

Posture — Standing

Perhaps you cross your arms in front of you or stand cross-legged. Perhaps all of your weight is on one leg while your knee is bent on the other. If you are a girl, perhaps you have high-heeled shoes on. All this is easily corrected, as posture for singing is simple. Stand with your feet shoulder width apart, hands by your sides, with relaxed shoulders. Your weight should be on the balls of the feet and slightly to the outside, and your knees should be unlocked, but not bent. It is important that your head remains level while singing. It should not be raised for high notes because this causes obstruction and constriction of the vocal cords, resulting in a thinner, less enchanting sound.

Five things you need to know in order to stand well and sing

Stand with your:

1. feet shoulder width apart

2. weight slightly on the balls of your feet and to the outsides

3. knees slightly bent

4. chest up

5. head level (chin not up).

High-heeled shoes should be avoided as they place the wrong emphasis on the supportive muscles of the larynx as well as throwing the pelvis forward. This causes the quadratus lumborum (the back muscles attached from the hip to the bottom rib) to pull on the latissimus dorsi (the back and side muscles that extend from the shoulder joint, across to the spine, and down to the hip).

They, in turn, can pull on the sterno cleido muscles, which run from the sternum bone (chest) to just behind your ears on both sides, tilting the larynx the wrong way.

The easiest way to ensure you have the correct posture is to watch yourself in a mirror as you sing. This way you can often correct any postural problems yourself. If you are observant, using a mirror will also give you the confidence to know you appear professional and relaxed in front of an audience.

Sitting down to sing while you play a musical instrument such as a guitar

1. Perhaps you play guitar and lean forward to sing into the microphone, thereby placing your head forward and you do not really make the strong sound you usually do. In this instance, always ensure, before you commence your performance, that you place the microphone where you need it, at the correct height for your own performance. Use a microphone stand that has a boom attached, i.e. one with an extension that can be adjusted for your height so that the boom reaches your mouth. This way your neck is not stretched forward and you can relax to perform.

2. Next you may think: "At home I sit on the floor and play my guitar without a strap. I practice my songs with my legs crossed and with my music lyrics on the floor in front of me. Is this a good thing?" The simple answer is: No, for several reasons. The muscles that support the vocal cords are stressed (restricted) and the air coming out is blocked when you look down to the floor. You will not make a good sound this way. Instead, use a music stand to keep your lyrics and chords at eye level. Either sit on a flat surface or a little forward on the seat, or you can stand up and use a music stand. You can use a drum or piano stool or flat chair. Do not sit right back on the surface. Come forward halfway and sit up straight. Now you are ready to make a good sound!

Closing your eyes

The minute you close your eyes, you tell your audience: "This performance is not for you". Remember to keep your eyes open at all times but if you are concerned about not being able to look at an audience, then focus your eyes on something somewhere just above eye level. This could be a spot on an audience member's head just above their eyes, such as between their eyebrows or on their forehead. You can work to that level throughout your performance as you work the room. Alternatively, you could focus on something on a wall and work that level all around the room. This reinforces that you are serious about what you are doing. As you look around, you involve the audience, telling them that your performance is for each and every single one of them. They then feel welcomed into your performance and will applaud you.

Singing up high one second and unable to reach lower notes the next

Take a minute here to consider a manual car gear stick. If you do not use the clutch, you grate the gears and execute a noticeable gear change. It is the same with the voice if you do not regularly practice scales to strengthen it. You must know which octaves you are singing in and develop a technique to involve all head (high) and chest (low) resonances, blending them until you can make the sounds from one register flow into another. I pull no punches here. This can take several years to develop, depending on how you apply yourself in regular practice sessions. The results, although elusive at first, are well worth the effort and pain you have to go through.

Another issue you will also need to look at is the key the

song is sung in. Does it suit your voice or do you feel uncomfortable and unsatisfied with your sound? There are certain keys better suited to a male than a female voice and vice versa. Even in gender, a soprano (high voice) will sing in a different key than a contralto (mid to lower range voice) and so on. In order to find the correct key for you, commit the song to memory and sing it in the register you are comfortable with. Then ask your musician to play it in your key, even if it is not necessarily the easiest for them. Together you will determine the right key for your voice for that particular song. It is okay if you cannot read music; just ask what key the song is played in and write down the song title and the key in a notebook. As time goes on, the entries in this notebook will grow, making it an invaluable tool in the future. This record will allow you to recall any song and key it is in at the drop of a hat.

Getting Started

You will be surprised at the results if you are able to apply a little discipline and organise your time. Begin to set up a weekly time frame to tell yourself what you are going to do and when. There may be times when you feel down and wonder why it is necessary to do all this "other stuff" just because of the need to sing one song really well. Keep on plodding and trust your vocal coach. You will be amazed at the progress you make when those six months are up and you have applied all the work given to you.

Just imagine that on the wedding or performance day, your song came out in tune, in time, wonderfully correct, delivered with emotion, plenty of breath for the phrases and everyone who commented said it was a wonderful performance! Yes! The room was spellbound. You could have heard a pin drop and although very nervous, your hard work paid off.

These are the kinds of results you can manage if you are diligent. It does not take the best singers to develop that kind of rapport with the audience. It takes the ones who work at it piece by piece until the puzzle comes together.

Regular singing practice will help you to be still inside. Daily deep breathing exercises will help relax your nervous system and improve your concentration and alertness. This will also help you become a much more confident singer, one that captures the listener's ear.

A singer's three best friends

A singer's three best friends are:

1. A mirror to carefully watch the position of your lips, tongue and jaw as you get to know the correct placement at all times and for all sounds.

2. A stopwatch to time breathing – a stopwatch is your lifelong friend.

3. Music stand to place music at the correct height.

After that comes the will to listen to yourself and distinguish the "right" way from the "wrong" way. Keep persisting and this will move you onwards. Always practice comfortably – not loudly. The importance of regular practice must be recognised and followed. You will improve after hours and hours of practice.

Next, sing a song you want to know and your practice will show and give you the honour of holding an audience's attention. Remember it is not the most wonderful sounding voice that wins in the end. It is the voice that regularly practices and applies the techniques of combined breathing, scales and diction.

Set goals

Keep a practice book at hand. Write in it your breathing, scales and times practiced. You will amaze yourself in three to six months' time with a vast improvement. You will be able to sing a strong and definite note, hold clear strong notes (up to 12 beats for some songs) and finish a song on a positive note!

I Can Sing, But Where is My Voice?

Practice — Breathing Exercises and Charts: the Daily Grind

Now that you know what you need to do to improve your singing, it is time to put all that theory into practice. Make time in your daily schedule to practice the basics of breathing, scales, exercises, long notes, and diction, and keep this up until you perform.

Do not sing when you have a sore throat, flu or similar illness. Wait until your speaking voice is back to normal and your energy levels are normal again.

Practice sessions

All practice sessions should consist of the following:

1. Deep breathing: 15 minutes. Advanced students 15 minutes three times a day.

2. Long notes: 15 to 20 minutes.

3. Scales and exercises: 25 to 30 minutes, initially. Advanced students up to two hours.

4. High and low resonance practice: humming or singing lines from your songs.

5. Songs: for as long as it takes.

Remember to use the mirror so you can keep your head level, check posture, and maintain the correct mouth placement for vowel sounds. Aim for clarity. It is also important to make sure you are relaxed before you practice. A good way to do this is to do three "screw ups" to prepare you for practice.

Prepare for practice

Preparation or "screw up" sessions should begin as follows:

1. Put on some easy listening music in the background very quietly, almost as if you have to strain to listen to it.

2. Lie down on a sofa, bed, or on the floor with a pillow to support your head.

3. Tighten up all the muscles in your body and hold for six seconds.

4. Release all the tension and completely relax for 40 seconds. Think about what it is you want out of life.

5. After your third "screw up", if you have not fallen asleep (some people do and that is okay), you should be ready to warm up for your practice.

Exercise 1.

Lie with your back as flat to the floor as is comfortable for you. Place your hands in the middle of your diaphragm (just above the belly button) with your two middle fingers touching. Take in a slow three second breath through the mouth, directing the air to the hard palate at the roof of your mouth. You should experience coolness on the roof of your mouth when the contact is correct. Blow out slowly and steadily. Listen to the air being expelled. Watch your stopwatch or clock. Try to exhale for one minute, blowing out through the smallest pinhole you can make with your lips. It may take months of daily practice to achieve one minute. To gauge your progress, record your times in a table like the one below.

Sample Breathing Chart for exercises 1 and 2

Attempt	Date	Blow out times achieved (in seconds)							
1									
2									
3									
4									
5									
6									
7									
8									
9									
10									

Attempt	Date	Blow out times achieved (in seconds)							
1									
2									
3									
4									
5									
6									
7									
8									
9									
10									

Attempt	Date	Blow out times achieved (in seconds)							
1									
2									
3									
4									
5									
6									
7									
8									
9									
10									

Excellent control — up to two minutes of exhaling — is usually reached in the first 12 months with regular daily practice four or more days a week. Work up to three daily 15 minute sessions.

Exercise 2.

This is applied when a regular 60 seconds of blowing out is reached in exercise 1.

Start by either standing up or lying flat on your back. Breathe in through your mouth for approximately three seconds, making sure to open your mouth wide while directing the air to the roof of your mouth. Before swallowing any air, exhale and verbally count out steadily without taking any breaths between numbers. You should aim to be able to count up to 30 at first before taking another breath. As you improve, you should be able to count to 60 in one minute – a good level for a modern song. You should be able to sing a 15 second phrase without taking a breath. This will make your song flow and ensure it is interesting to the listener's ear.

To practice, take a line from your song and speak it first. Ensure words that start with a vowel are clear. For example, if your song contains a line such as: "And I love you," make sure the, "a" and the "I" are crisp and clear, and then make sure you apply that when singing.

Using a Glottal Stroke

Glottal strokes are generally used when singing a vowel sound. Below are a few hints to help you achieve the correct mouth position for each of these vowel sounds. Use a scale and practice these sounds up and down the scale. Keep your mouth in the same position (i.e. do not close your mouth or change your lip position).

A Always sing this with a flat tongue and your mouth wide open. Try a "three finger drop" by inserting your fingers between the top and bottom rows of teeth. It should sound like "ae".

E Try to sing it with a smile.

I Drop the jaw and do not close it until the short or long "i" sound is finished.

O Perform this with rounded lips, a glottal stroke, and hold the position until the sound is completed. If you change the lip position during execution, what will be heard will be "o-u" rather than "o".

U This should sound like "oo", with lips rounded rather like a fish coming up for air.

Vowel Pronunciation

Rules to remember when pronouncing a vowel are:

1. Commence with the correct jaw position.

2. Start each vowel with a glottal stroke. This gives clarity to the words you are pronouncing.

3. Train the tongue to lie flat.

4. When singing any of the vowel sounds, hold your mouth position until the end of delivery (i.e. until the sound is finished), and then close your mouth.

Practice these rules and glottal strokes in front of a mirror. Remember to over emphasise the sounds using a wider opening of the mouth, flat tongue, and correct position for the lips. Mastering this should help you solve the problem of using breath before tone and give your pronunciation clarity so that the listener can hear acceptable diction and melody.

Sounds to Practice

Around the time you begin to perfect your practice of vowels with clarity, it is a good idea to introduce the use of all sounds. The shape of your mouth will change the sounds surrounding a vowel, depending on what letters precede or follow it.

For example, "i" is sung as follows:

1. Drop the jaw with your tongue flat.

2. Say the "i".

3. Finish the "i".

4. Close the jaw.

All this is done in a split second using the muscles of the face and jaw. A correctly produced "i" is very clear to the listener's ear. However, the same exercise cannot be used for the "i" in the word "coming". The "i" sound becomes almost a closed mouth position.

Some practice exercises that can help

The following are some exercises to develop confidence when you learn to sing all kinds of words in different songs. You will come across many words you do not use in everyday life. But being able to confidently sing them will help you stay more relaxed and focused. This will enhance your ability to deliver an acceptable song that is pleasing to the listener's ear.

Practice the following sounds. Make sure you use the correct position of the lips and jaw and take a diaphragmatic breath. To hear the sound clearly, cup your hand over your ear, bending the top of your ear forward.

Oh — ah — ee and Oh — no — woe

If you do not position the lips carefully and consciously – an "o-shape" for the "o" sound, mouth wide for the "a" and a wide smile for the "e" – the sound will be dull. It is a good idea to sing it both the right and the wrong way to hear the difference. Watch yourself in the mirror and practice with your mouth open in the correct position. Listen for clarity.

If you do it correctly, you will hear a clearer sound. If you do it wrong, the sound will be dull and hard to comprehend. Try again going slowly down and up the scale in semi-tones (half notes). Use some form of glottal stroke on the vowels, whether it is a subtle or more pronounced one.

Sai lee — ai lee

Remember the basic position for "a" with tongue flat and mouth open wide and remember to smile the "e" sound. Go downscale in semi-tones and back up again. When you first start, one octave at a time is plenty to do up and down the scale. Gradually increase to two then three octaves as your range develops.

Evermore

Try to sing "evermore" by beginning with a glottal stroke and a slightly longer emphasis on the first "e". Remember to smile. Round the lips for the "ver" sound, and then close the lips for the "m" and open to a circle for the "ore". From this you can see there are three positions for the lips. Try it slowly at first in three syllables, and then proceed by semi-tones down and up the scale. Do it softly at first.

Up pup

In one second, drop the jaw for "u" and push out the first "p" with a gentle blowing which extends the "p" sound. Then pronounce "pup". Make sure all of the "p" sounds are clear, ensuring the "p" sounds at the end of "up" and "pup" are pushed out with a puff. If you do not pronounce the third "p", your words will not sound clear.

I cry, high sky, my my, why I? I try

This is a good exercise to get the feel for annunciating an "i" sound. Remember to drop the jaw for all of the phrases that begin with an "i" sound and for the "y" in "my". This can be hard work for the muscles of the jaw and mouth, but you will reap good results for clarity if you do these on one note at a time. Make sure not to close the jaw too soon because this will introduce another sound to the vowel, giving it an "i-ee" sound. Remembering to keep the jaw down a fraction longer before closing it is all it takes.

Cookoo cookoo coo caw caw caw
(sounds like "cook-koo")

This is a good exercise to clear unwanted mucus from the back of your throat. Try it in semi-tones, up and down the scale for 15 minutes. Remember to round your lips for the "o" sound.

Around the time you begin to perfect your practice of vowels with clarity it is a good idea to introduce the use of all sounds.

Physical Warm-Ups

Physical warm-ups are a good idea before any performance or practice session. They will help you perform to the best of your ability and can also prevent injury. Below are some physical exercises that every singer needs.

Neck muscles

Stand tall with your feet shoulder width apart. Lift both arms outwards. Keep them level, and move them round and round. Do five circles one way then five the other way. Repeat this three times. Let them gently fall to your sides when tired.

Voice and neck

Stand in front of a mirror. Drop your chin to your chest. Keep your shoulders down. Slowly commence head circles. Rotate first to the left until a full circle is completed, then rotate to the right. Repeat this several times over a period of 10 minutes. This exercise helps loosen the muscles of the neck and will relax the larynx.

To relax the muscles at the root of the tongue

Gently tilt your head backwards and hold this position. Drop the jaw slowly to the count of three. Gradually close the jaw to the slow count of five and hold it closed for five seconds. Relax. Repeat the exercise five times.

How to Practice

Finally, it is time to get into your practice. The following are some examples of practice sessions for people at different levels of singing proficiency.

Beginners' practice session

1. Start with breathing exercises: 10 minutes a day.

2. Scales and warm-ups in front of a mirror: 15 to 20 minutes, five days a week.

3. Lastly, add your songs and practice them.

Intermediate practice session

1. Deep breathing exercises: 15 minutes twice a day, writing down your times.

2. Scales, long notes, and exercises in front of a mirror: 45 minutes to one hour, five days a week.

3. Songs: as long as it takes (hours).

Well developed student practice session

1. Deep breathing exercises: three 20 minute sessions a day.

2. Scales, long notes, and exercises: two hours, five days a week.

3. Songs: as it takes (over and over).

Why do I have to do boring scales and exercises when all I want to do is sing a good song?

The simple answer is that scales and exercises (both vocal and physical) strengthen your voice and help you sing in tune, if done on a daily basis. They improve the clarity of the notes you wish to express.

Scales can be boring, but if you watch how you do them in a mirror and how you slowly begin to "own" each note you sing, the results can be very rewarding. Of course, you have to forget them to sing a song, but once in the sub-conscious, they stay there and produce a pleasing result for an audience.

The majority of the assessment problems point to the need to practice breathing to control the air coming out of your mouth for a smooth sound. There is a need to practice deep breathing daily, along with vowel pronunciation, resonance, scales, and long notes. If you practice softly, the voice strengthens bit by bit. Loud practice can damage the delicate tissues of the throat and oral cavities and is not necessarily good practice. One misplaced scream or shout can burst a blood vessel in the throat and cause permanent damage.

Choosing Which Songs Suit Your Voice

Choosing the type of music that is best suited to your voice is an important part of ensuring your performance is the best it can be. A good way to do this is to carry out the following exercise to better understand yourself and where you would like to go with your music choice. It is all about what you feel when you listen to any given piece of music.

First, gather up as many CDs and songs of your favourite artists as possible. Ask your friends and family if you can borrow any of the ones you do not have, or go to the library and select artists from various categories. It is a good idea to use at least 20 to 50 singers for this exercise, giving yourself two to three days to listen and write down some comments. Make notes, listing the singer and the song, and assess which songs you like based on the following:

Diction	Could I understand the words?
Breathing	Was the breathing noisy or quiet?
Knowledge of Scales	Was the whole song in tune?
Feeling	Was there expression? Did it feel like it came from the heart?

Control of air	How long was it before the artist took a breath? It should be between eight and fifteen seconds between breaths, depending on the length of the phrases.
Resonance	Was the gear change between high and low notes noticeable or fluid? Did it sound like there were two different singers in the same song?
Power	Is this singer using their diaphragm?

There will be some artists you love and others you dislike. Make notes on this. Try to sing along to the ones you enjoy most. If you have trouble singing in the same key as an artist, the song may need to be played in a different key for your voice. If you do not play an instrument, the best way to find out the key you are singing in is to sing the songs you like to a musician friend or teacher and ask them to give you the key. Make sure the musician fits his or her chords to your voice, not the other way around. Write down the key next to the song title in your notes. By doing this, you may find that your voice is best suited to a particular genre.

Is your voice best suited to:

1. Pop

2. Rock or rock 'n' roll

3. Motown Ballads

4. Easy listening middle of the road (MOR)

5. Jazz – standards or Latin

6. Heavy metal

7. Blues or Reggae

8. Spiritual or Gospel

9. Folk

10. Country or country cross or rock

11. Musical shows or theatre?

There are many other categories, but the above list is a good start.

Performance on the Day

Nerves will abound, but that is normal. The finest performers also get butterflies. Here are some tried and true ways to help keep you calm on your big day.

1. Make sure the day before the performance is a relaxed day, all about you. No singing, yelling, or talking excitedly. It is quiet time all day. Get a good eight hours sleep and prepare everything you will need including music, microphone, PA system, sound check, and clothes. At sound check, ensure you have a monitor speaker at your feet as it is often hard to hear yourself over the musicians. Make sure your clothes are ready and set out, shoes cleaned, and you are spotless for the day of the performance. Be organised!

2. If you have time on the day of the performance, it is a good idea to get yourself a massage. This massage should encompass head, neck, shoulders, back, as well as intercostal muscles. One hour spent having a good massage will be invaluable for your song delivery. It will centre you, relax the muscles you need to work with, and you will sing like a bird. Make sure your massage person uses only cold-pressed natural oils. Almond oil with a few drops of lavender is excellent and will prove very calming. If almond oil is unavailable, then apricot oil can be used. It is not advisable to use synthetic oils because the body cannot absorb them. If you are singing in the morning, it is a good idea to have a massage in the afternoon or evening the day before. If you are singing

in the evening, get a massage in the morning on the day. To find an ethical masseuse, refer to the Australian College of Massage (ACM) whose practitioners are fully registered and accredited for therapeutic and relaxation massage.

3. A word about cigarettes, drugs, tattoos and alcohol. Do not go there. They break the body's natural biochemistries and rob you of the much needed mucus attached to delicate nasal and vocal passages. You need these mucus linings intact to be able to do your job well. You will get far more positive things happening for your body without the use of cigarettes, drugs, tattoos and alcohol. If you have practiced and know your song, this is the time to have faith in yourself and trust that you will do a pleasing performance because you have put in all the ground work.

4. Make sure you bring a positive and bubbly attitude to your performance. Leave your troubles at the door. The audience does not want to know about the negative experiences in your life; they are there to see you and hear you sing. A good exercise to help you forget your troubles is to close your eyes. Imagine a door, open it and enter into a room filled with your favourite calming colour, closing the door behind you. Think of something you really want to achieve in life or be in a place you want to be. This will relax you.

5. Two days before the performance, organise your diet to exclude foods such as white flour, sugar products, and dairy (cheese, cow's milk, yoghurt, and fatty or greasy foods). These products create mucus and can cause a post nasal drip that blocks your lovely high notes from coming out. Replace these foods with plenty of fresh vegetables, fruit, lean cuts

of meat, tofu, chicken, fish or vegetarian meals. Also, do not eat a big meal just before a performance.

6. Drink six to eight glasses of water a day. If you have trouble with mucus, an early morning gargle of sea or celtic salt (one teaspoon in warm water) can help. Unsweetened pineapple juice or fresh pineapple works well for thinning nasal mucus and can be taken up to 15 minutes before the show.

7. Find a quiet spot 20 minutes before you are about to perform and take three long deep breaths. This will help settle your nerves and centre you for your performance. At some point during the final hour, make sure to do 15 minutes of scales to warm up your vocal chords.

8. When the time comes to perform, make sure to put all of your heart into your performance. Do not just be a parrot. Tell the story. Be ready to share and express the emotion of your song to the audience. Making the audience feel your performance gives it credibility. It cannot be taught to you. It comes from your heart and an honest desire to make the best of what you know.

Microphone Technique

You may think singing with a microphone looks straightforward, but there are a few things to learn if you want to make your performance the best it can be.

How to hold a microphone

Pick up the microphone and place your thumb on the band around its middle. Wrap your fingers gently around so that you have control from the wrist, not your shoulder. When you are singing your song, the microphone should be held about five centimetres from your lips and down slightly so that your mouth may be seen while you are performing. Another thing to note is that you should never blow into a microphone as this can damage it. If you need to check the volume, use words such as: "Testing, one, two, three".

Buying a microphone (and other useful equipment)

There are several different types of microphones available today. Among the most reliable for popular performers is the Shure SM58 and others in the Shure range. There are several different types of microphones available today. The SM58 is a unidirectional microphone and can pick up sound best from the top. Decent uni-directional microphones can be purchased in Australia for around $200 and upwards and are much better than other types of microphones used for speaking. If you are a professional singer, buying your own public address (PA) system is another excellent investment. If you can find the Shure brand, all the better. If not, other brands such as Yorkville, Behringer, and Mackie and many others are available. A PA system is an expensive purchase. But getting the sound that works for you all the time will save you a lot of stress and anxiety.

Look after your equipment

It is important to look after any equipment you own if you want it to have a long life. Put it away when not in use and it will last a long time. Make sure you have covers for speakers and sponge lining to keep microphones in. An SM58 will last up to 20 years if well kept. Rules like: "No drinks or cigarettes on the speakers or amps," will save you thousands of dollars in maintenance.

Frequently Asked Questions

Should I sing if I have a cold, flu, sore throat, or asthma?

No. During this time, infected mucus and swelling prevent vocal notes from entering the oral cavities. Enlarged tonsils also interfere with the sound you make. If you do sing, you risk damage to your vocal chords. Sometimes this damage can be permanent. It is best to rest and sing only when your speaking voice is back to normal.

How do I sing clean and clear notes that people will enjoy listening to?

This all comes from using pressure from the diaphragm and breathing as you have been shown. It is important to use upper (head) and lower (chest) resonance. Shape your lips correctly for the given sound and open your mouth wider than for everyday speech. This will help your sound carry a long way.

How do I sing a smooth note?

The best way to master this is to practice singing long notes. You should aim to reach 25 seconds singing a vowel sound. Keep your mouth in the correct position as you sing the note and use a glottal stroke. Aim at first to hold a note for eight beats, then 12, 16 and finally 32 beats. All of this takes a lot of practice. When you first start practicing long notes, it is a good idea, to start again every time you wobble, until you can make it smooth.

What preparation should I do before I go on stage to sing?

Make sure you arrive early, well before the time of your performance, and do some calming exercises.
Half-an-hour before you are due to sing, you should:

1. Find a quiet spot somewhere.

2. Offer a prayer for guidance (if you are spiritual).

3. Take three deep breaths.

4. Sing some scales for 15 minutes.

5. Be happy and forget your troubles for now.

When you are performing, make sure to keep your eyes open. Bodily movement is fine, but make sure to involve the audience and be relaxed.

What is vibrato?

Vibrato is a pulsation of pitch accompanied by a simultaneous pulsation of loudness and timbre. Pitch can pulsate between five and eight times a second. If it occurs fast, it becomes a bleat. If it occurs slowly, it is heard as a wobble.

Generally vibrato is not lauded by the audiences of contemporary or popular singers. If you must use it, do so sparingly.

My voice breaks after singing. What is wrong?

This usually occurs when you force the sounds from your throat while singing. Remember that the sounds you sing must be caused solely by the breath from the diaphragm using the correct higher or lower resonances. They must not be forced. The muscles at the root of the tongue and jaw must be relaxed and your head should remain level (do not raise it) when singing high notes.

What are the basic mouth positions for the vowels?

A   Sing with a flat tongue, a smile and with your mouth in a three finger drop.
E   Sing it with a smile.
I   Drop the jaw, sing the sound, finish the sound, close the jaw. This takes about one second.
O   Jaw dropped half way, lips out in an "o" shape.
U   Push rounded lips out. Should sound like "oo" and look like a fish.

When singing, the mouth is opened much wider than for everyday speech. This gives clarity to the listener's ear. Remember to commence with the correct mouth position. Start each vowel with some form of glottal stroke and train the tongue to lie flat. When singing any of the vowel sounds, add a short 'e' to the end of the sound (not a long one). Hold your mouth position until the end of delivery (i.e. until the sound is finished), and then close your mouth.

Where do singers get their power from?

Singers get their power from a combination of deep breathing, scales, and the use of correct resonance and diction. It may take you many months of practice to achieve, but the results are rewarding for both you and your audience.

What will it take to be a confident singer?

The answer to this is practice, practice, practice. You should do breathing, scales, diction and long note practice regularly for at least an initial six to twelve month period. You will also need to learn all three octaves of pitch and be able to use all 37 notes of your three octave range. Also, know the words of your song before you sing. This is important.

How long will it take before I can get my mouth to make the sounds I really want it to?

The time it takes to learn to sing varies between people. Some people can reach a relatively high level in six to twelve months, while others take five years or more. To get your singing voice to a level where you can sing any song and people will like it can take up to seven years of hard work and fine-tuning.

Sometimes when I sing a song, I sing up high one minute and down low the next. What is happening?

1. Check the key you are trying to sing in is right for you. It may be too high or too low. Often sheet music will need to be adjusted for different voices.

2. Have you had 15 minutes of warm-ups before you started singing? Practicing breathing and scales before you go on stage is very important and will make a big difference to your performance.

What does singing flat mean?

Singing flat usually means that you are:

1. Forcing air out instead of letting it out.

2. Restricting the larynx and tightening the muscle at the root of the tongue (you will see strap muscles standing out in the neck like small veins). They need to be very relaxed.

3. Not listening to scales and need more practice.

4. Still learning to develop high resonance.

Did you know?

Anyone can learn to sing as long as they are not physically deaf. However, it will take each person a different length of time to do so.

Question Time

Test yourself

If you can answer the following questions correctly, good progress has been made. You are ready to make an informed start for better singing.

1. When you sing, do you breathe through your mouth or nose?

2. Can you use your nose to breathe in for singing?

3. Where do you breathe to and from?

4. What muscles do you use?

5. If you are going to sing while sitting down, what is the best way to sit?

6. Should you raise your head when singing a high note?

7. Should you move your head while singing?

8. Where should you look when singing to an audience?

9. How do you sing a high note?

10. How should you breathe for singing?

11. What is the best way to control your breath?

12. What is important for good diction (pronunciation)?

13. Can you perform a glottal stroke?

14. What microphone do I use and how do I hold it?

15. How do I sing high notes?

16. What does resonance mean?

17. What is good posture for a singer?

18. What do you need to do to prepare for a stage performance?

19. Should you sing if you have a sore throat, cold, or flu?

20. Can you correct all 11 of the problems listed in 'Assessment'?

21. What is the best way to practice?

22. Does it matter if you cannot read music?

23. What do you need to know if you cannot read music?

24. How do you strengthen your voice?

25. Should you practice scales as often as you practice your songs?

26. Does smoking affect a singer?

27. Is listening important if you want to sing in tune?

28. How can you hold a long note without running out of breath?

29. What do you need to do in order to have a powerful voice?

30. What could a possible reason be for your throat hurting after singing for a while?

31. How can you stop yourself from running out of breath a lot?

32. How can you know whether you are singing in tune or not, and how can you fix it?

33. How can you make sure you do not sing unwanted notes in front of the ones you want to sing (i.e. slurring or scooping)?

34. What do you need to do to make high notes sound good and preserve your voice?

35. Why is it important to know all 37 notes of the three octaves?

36. Why do you need to open your mouth wide, use your lips, and keep your tongue flat?

37. What can you do to make it easier to hear yourself sing when the band is really loud?

38. Will my singing sound good if the muscle at the root of my tongue is tense?

39. Do you need to sing loud all the time?

40. What does it mean when people say you need to be still inside when you sing?

(For answers go to page 104.)

Students' Stories

Are you wondering if you can sing?

Here are some inspiring stories from students who have plucked up the courage to go to singing lessons. Many of them went in with little or no formal training but managed to come out six months to a year later with the courage to fulfil their singing dreams.

Savannah, 23, Wellington

From the very start my teacher was exuberant. She was thorough and created an interest in the theoretical side of singing. With this newly found know-how, I discovered an enthusiasm for practice I had never had before and my voice became much stronger.

I joined a band at work as the lead singer, even though I had only played instruments in bands in the past. At this stage, I had only been to a few lessons with my new teacher and I was still very nervous. Fortunately, after following all of my teacher's instructions thoroughly on a daily basis, I was able to pull off the role with pizzazz and strength. My stage performance was beyond anything that I had ever thought I could achieve.

The breathing exercises I had been learning at practice began to integrate themselves into my daily life as well. I could talk for longer in one breath, I took up swimming on a daily basis, and I even started doing the exercises while I was working in graphic design at the movie studios. After a while I started to form stomach muscles I never knew I had. The vowel and pronunciation exercises helped to give my general speaking voice a new clarity and strength, which was even noticeable to other people.

After a while, I became so keen on the exercises that I would take my stopwatch to bed at night at the end of a stressful day at work. The breathing exercises I had learned in practice helped me to wind down and relax and I slept better than ever. I really enjoyed how my modern teacher's tried and true methods were so holistic and incorporated exercise, health, breathing, pronunciation, clean living, and relaxation. In the end, I gained much more than just singing ability; I felt and looked more confident and happy overall.

Ben, in his 20s, Wellington

Before getting vocal lessons, I had what I would term a "meat and potatoes" kind of voice. I could hold a tune, but felt limited in how I could use my voice. I really was not sure how to improve.

In just a couple of lessons, I began to notice the difference that working on my breathing and vowel pronunciation made. My voice has quickly become stronger and clearer and I feel like I have much more control over it. I used to have good days and bad days and not really know why. Now if I am having an off day, I have a whole lot of things that I can check on. I ask myself: "Am I breathing from my stomach, not my chest? Am I opening my mouth wide enough and forming the words properly? Have I warmed up properly?" Having the knowledge to fix what I am doing wrong makes me feel more confident when performing in public and this helps both my vocal tone and my overall performance.

Sandey, 35, Wellington

I was experiencing dramatic changes in my life when I began singing lessons in October of 1999. I had always wanted to sing in front of others, but for one reason or another, I just had not got around to it. Learning to sing properly was one thing I just had to do. The lessons were fantastic. I gained so much technical knowledge in just a few months and learned how to practice properly with breathing and scales.

I felt a real sense of improvement in my voice and after only three months of lessons, I got a singing part in a play with just a piano to accompany me. This was a huge confidence boost for me and something I would never have had the courage to do without any lessons.

Leonie, 30, Wellington

I have always loved to sing, much to the disgust of my brother. Usually it was with a hairbrush singing to the mirror in my room as a child. "Oh my ears!" was always the cry from down the hall.

Despite the lack of faith my brother had in my performances, I made it into the school choir and continued to sing all through university. Although many of my friends and teachers commented on my ability, I never went far with it because I did not want to be thought of as a show-off.

Then one summer, I was singing around the fire with some friends and someone said: "Wow, you can really sing". I had just left my partner at the time and hit 30 years of age. I decided then and there that the time was right to finally inquire about lessons.

I made an appointment with a teacher and I was so nervous.

The day of my lesson I am sure I did not do any work at all. When I turned up at the teacher's address, I sat in my car for 10 minutes before going in to see her. We had a chat about what I wanted to do and I sheepishly said: "I do not know. I just wanted to give it a go." She understood. We did a few scales and she taught me some breathing techniques. I knew nothing about music and notes or anything – it was all quite daunting.

I persisted with the lessons and I gained a whole lot of confidence. Singing in front of other people is not a problem anymore. I do daily breathing exercises and scales, and I have invested in a small electric keyboard. I still do not know exactly what I want to do with music, but the more I do it, the more I love it. I think we take music for granted in the good times. You find yourself tapping your foot to a tune on the radio and you do not notice it is actually making you happier. It is not until you are down in the dumps that you realise how comforting music can be.

Keith, in his 50s, Rotorua

I decided to take singing lessons after playing the piano accordion for about 40 years. Although I often sang when I played, I really wanted to know if I was singing in tune or if I would be able to hold notes.

I imagine I was something of a problem to a singing tutor. I would arrive for my lesson and proceed to strap 12 kilograms of metal and plastic to my chest in the form of a piano accordion. This inhibited my ability to breathe properly and made the achievements I had gained from breathing practice difficult to reproduce at lesson time. Remembering the words of the song was also extremely difficult while playing the unwieldy accordion. After weeks of persevering, we decided that the best bet would be to learn to sing first and then play the accordion at the same time later on. We did this and I began to make steady progress as the year moved on.

I finished my year of lessons happy with the progress I had made. Much of my time involved learning to breathe properly and to think about the song I was going to sing before starting. I still play the accordion and sing along, but now I can finally hold the tune. I am grateful for my teacher's encouragement and patience.

Mary-Sue, in her 30s, Upper Hutt

It had long been my dream to get involved in amateur musical theatre, but upon attending my first audition, I was not accepted for any part. Feeling slightly downhearted, I decided that if I was going to be serious about singing, I had better receive some vocal coaching.

I took lessons for more than a year before I had the confidence to try for another show. When I finally did, it was for a place in the chorus of a classic rock 'n' roll theatre show called, 'Be Bop A Lu La!' To my amazement, I was offered the lead. It took 24 hours for my feet to come down to the ground again. I was ecstatic.

Taking singing lessons has done some amazing things for my self-confidence. I always thought I had a nice voice, but now I know that others think so too. I attribute the achievement of my goal to learning how to breathe for singing, practicing scales so that I can hit my target note, and learning what a glottal stroke is and how to apply it.

Probably the greatest influence, however, was the time spent with an excellent vocal coach who helped me see where I was going wrong. She was a great motivator, giving me exercises and feedback, which I worked on independently.

Jim, 40, Tauranga

I came up with this crazy idea in a flurry of romantic love that I would surprise my bride-to-be and melt her heart by singing on our wedding day. The only problem was that I was not a singer. I could not start a song in tune or hold the tune at all.

Needless to say, when the reality of singing in public loomed large, I was tempted to flag it away as just a crazy idea. But the thought of seeing Laurelle's face in shock and awe kept the idea simmering in my mind. Laurelle is a very good singer, having led her own bands and led singing in the churches she attended over the years.

I had decided to sing a wedding song called 'How Fine it Seems to Me' written by the Celtic artist Sammy Horner. My intention was to have a friend who played the guitar come up and stand beside me just after we had exchanged vows so I could sing to Laurelle. My problem was I did not know of a teacher. It was then that I contacted a lady who was a member of Rotorua's Saint John's In the City. I was the minister at the time.

With encouragement and skill she took a virtually tone deaf nervous 40-year-old and helped hone a voice that passed on the day. It took six months of regular lessons learning voice and listening exercises to recognise the right notes as well as breathing exercises to deal with nerves and the mechanics of projecting my voice. I had my friend record the song onto a tape so I could practice while driving the car.

If I can be taught to sing, anyone can. Seeing the surprise on Laurelle's face and her eyes glisten with tears of joy and love as I sang on our wedding day was worth the nerves and the practice. The guests even gave me a round of applause. They were so surprised and moved. Thanks to my teacher's skill and encouragement, I can now sing in tune and start a song pretty well. May the benefits continue.

Leo, in his 20s, Wellington

My desire to sing was fuelled by the various performers I admired. Their individual styles and ideas convinced me that everyone has the opportunity to express their own unique flavour through singing.

Like a lot of skills, singing seemed to come to me so slowly that I did not notice myself progressing. The skills I acquired through lessons and practice were worked for every inch of the way. I found that I had to have a lot of faith in myself while practicing, assuring myself that the strained voice coming from my throat would improve as time went on.

By the end of my lessons, I had improved hugely. I discovered that any notion that singing is something you are born with or is a natural gift should be thrown out the window. The world's best performers did not come in off the street and start warbling; they studied, practiced, and worked hard to become who they are. Everyone has to start somewhere. Hard work is all it takes.

Helen, late 20s, Rotorua

When I started taking singing lessons in my late 20s, I was stressed to the max. I was uptight, nervous, and prone to the type of shallow breathing that tends to make your body more acidic than is healthy.

Vocal training taught me the importance of deep rhythmic diaphragmatic breathing. Although I had practiced other methods of breath control, particularly with karate training, it was the daily systemic practice of extending the diaphragm to breathe that brought great benefits to my life. I became more relaxed, centring my energy in the mid-region of my body rather than my chest, and I developed more power and control for my singing voice. My confidence and clarity of thought improved remarkably, genuinely helping in the recent writing and production of my first music album.

Andrew, 28, Wellington

The desire to sing is as instinctive for humans as it is for birds. Unfortunately, as humans, we feel embarrassed if we believe our ability is below par. For me, getting singing lessons was about gaining an understanding of my voice so that my confidence could match my desire to sing. The hardest thing was finding a comfortable space to practice. I lacked the confidence to practice when others were around. My solution was to sing my scales in the car while I was travelling. It was not ideal, but it gave me the space I needed until I was ready to share my voice. I do, however, have a word of warning for those who think this is a good idea. Make sure your phone is off! During a long drive recently, I bumped my cell phone and left my friend a long voice message of me singing along to Metallica. Luckily he has a good sense of humour and deleted it without sharing it with the rest of my friends.

    I was not blessed with a naturally beautiful voice and even after lessons, I am not about to enter 'New Zealand Idol'. What I have gained from my time with a singing teacher is a whole lot of understanding. I now know what suits my range and timbre and I can sing when and where I know it will provide me with the most enjoyment. My words of advice are – do not give up, love your unique voice, and have fun with it!

Shelley, 31, Wellington

As a teenager I sang at weddings, in musicals, and I was part of a choir. The singing ceased once I joined the workforce, but the passion returned last year after I was introduced to the angelic voice of Eva Cassidy.

I embarked on eight months of lessons with my teacher, working on diction, breathing, posture, scale range, and learning how to take care of myself. It was hard work, but I quickly realised the importance of practice. The transition from learning to sing a song to actually feeling the song did not occur overnight, but when the penny dropped, it was incredible. The lessons gave me the confidence to try new things and I began adding my own interpretation to songs.

Recently, I have taken up guitar lessons, which have enabled me to write my own material. I have really begun to flourish as a singer songwriter. I still cannot believe that at 31, I am fulfilling a childhood dream. With the right amount of encouragement, support, guidance, and passion, the world really can be your oyster.

Jess, 17, Wellington

I have always been quite the performer and have enjoyed singing since I was a little girl. I remember vaguely that my first real performance was in front of a big crowd at my auntie's wedding when I was four. Instead of saying a few words, as the flower girl usually does, I sung Michael Jackson's, 'Heal the World'.

Before going to lessons, I had been involved in school choirs, barbershops, Kapa Haka and school musicals. Neither of my parents could sing and it was always a mystery where I got my voice from. My mum used to joke that it must have been from the thousands of times I watched Julie Andrews in *Mary Poppins* when I was a three year old.

My singing teacher helped me become aware of what was important in singing and taught me that it is more than opening your mouth and making a noise. I found the one-on-one teaching very rewarding and I learned quickly what I personally needed to know to get better.

I gained the skills and confidence to take my performances out of my home and onto the big stage, singing a solo performance of, 'The Game of Love,' in front of 20,000 people at Wellington's Carols by Candlelight. I also entered a number of competitions and concerts which have been very rewarding. Getting up on stage and sharing a little bit of myself with my audience is something I love. I plan to go to university to study contemporary music and performing arts, before writing my own songs and pursuing a career in music.

Benjamin, 27, Wellington

Since I was young I have enjoyed singing with my family and in churches. During high school, I sung for the main choir. My ambition had always been to develop my singing ability to clearly express my passion and maximise my life.

I had taken some voice training lessons in the past, but they did not seem to help greatly. When a friend told me about a teacher she had heard great things about, I jumped at the chance.

I booked a lesson and turned up at the teacher's house. She

was warm and welcoming. What really blew me away was how I felt very relaxed to open everything up so that I could learn and develop.

At first it was basic scales and songs to develop my pitch. I found this difficult at first but developed quickly, enjoying this work. I also had to do some weird exercises for my breathing. I had to learn to control it, to make sure I was not letting air out quickly. When I started work on my pronunciation of songs, she made me pay attention to the detail of each part of the songs, my breathing, pitch, and timing. I learned to sing a song bit by bit, making sure I got it right. This taught me a lot, not only for my singing, but about life in general. I needed to pay attention to each detail to produce the required outcome.

At later sessions, I began to learn about the correct posture for singing. I had a bad habit of lifting my head as the pitch of the song went up. It took me a long time to get this right, especially when the mirror was not in front of me and I was really passionate about a song!

Fiona, 31, Wellington

I wanted to find a singing teacher who was contemporary as I did not feel that a classical teacher could help me. For months I looked on websites and in the yellow pages searching for the teacher who was right for me. I found many, some with glowing testimonials and pictures, but I judged them without meeting them, thinking they had nothing to offer me. I had been singing since I was a kid and had won two talent quests. Surely I knew more than most of them, I thought.

Although my attendance has been very sporadic over the past few years, what I have learned is worth its weight in gold. My singing lessons helped me improve my breathing and showed me a technique to improve my higher range. I can especially remember hearing that people must understand every word.

Since the lessons, I have achieved many things I never dreamed of. I won a song writing competition in 2003. I auditioned for the Auckland Christmas in the Park, and I recently celebrated my 31st birthday with my own concert for family and friends.

Your Health As A Singer

Staying healthy is as important for a singer as it is for any professional athlete. Athletes need to be fit if they want to avoid injury and remain competitive, and singers need to remain healthy if they want to have a powerful voice that is usable for most of their lives. For both the singer and the athlete, good health is vital to a successful career.

The most basic precaution you can take to look after your wellbeing as a singer is to maintain a healthy diet.

You should eat plenty of fruit and salad and drink six to eight large glasses of water a day. This will give you drive and stamina.

By eating organically grown fruit and vegetables you can enjoy a healthy diet as well as the flavour of your food. Pesticides leave food bland and tasteless. Sue Kedgley's *Eating safely in a toxic world* is a most informative book in this regard and can help you to make wise choices for your future health.

Daily exercise is important too. A healthy body means a healthy mind. If you want to remain healthy and ensure your singing voice remains strong, make sure you get outdoors and do at least four hours of exercise every week, even if it is only walking. Also, always remember to take pride in your personal appearance and hygiene. This will help you avoid offending your audience and people around you.

The Voice, The Popular Song, And The Singer

By Peter Blake, MA, MB, BS, FRACS, Otolaryngologist and head and neck surgeon.

Let us step back and spend a moment or two just thinking about the title of this article. We are talking here about a relatively new phenomenon and that is, taking the popular song and its voice seriously. I do not mean to say that Frank Sinatra or Elvis Presley or even Sir Mick Jagger did not have a singing teacher and did not spend time on technique. But the traditional popular singer has in the past been largely untaught.

It is the classical voice that has received all of the attention in terms of general bodily health, breathing technique, posture, warm-up techniques, and a very studied view about what is an acceptable amount of singing over a period of time. The culture of the pop song has been very much more "get up and do it". It is part of being "cool".

From a voice point of view, a revisit is long overdue. The popular voice can no longer be relegated to second place and, in any event, the boundaries between the classically trained voice and the popular voice have become increasingly blurred. Andrea Bocelli's, 'Romanza,' was a defining point in the evolution of the blend between the popular and classical voice. There have been others before him but the commercial success of his classical approach to popular singing cannot be denied. It is not to say that one can look at the Bocelli approach and say it works for the rock singer. It does not.

If we talk about the health of the voice, we think about general bodily health, and we think about the respiratory organs – the lungs, the diaphragm, the upper airway, the nose, mouth, and throat. We think about posture, breathing, and technique. You know where we end up.

Point one. There is much you can learn from the classical voice technique in terms of posture, breathing, and projection techniques but, remember, you are not a classical singer. Your world – its culture, and its technology – is different.

Point two. How is it different? The differences are (a) the environment (b) the culture and (c) the technology.

a) The environment

This is a hang loose environment in which you do your thing. Whilst a classical singer pushes the envelope in terms of technique, this occurs within very well-defined boundaries. For you, there are no rules, there are no boundaries, and the limit is constantly pushed. The bottom line is that you push the envelope. The corollary of this is that you must create the boundaries yourself. If you do not, you are going to run into vocal problems. What are your limits? You must have some idea of just how much singing you can do, at what volume, and over what range. If you belt out for five hours a night in a pub for seven days a week, you will have vocal problems.

b) **The culture**

The environment is different. You are not singing on a stage with a large orchestra in front of a load of boring old farts. You are singing in front of an audience that is relaxed, casual, and looking for fun and entertainment. Your audience is not quiet. It does not tolerate five minutes of the composer deciding he and everybody else need a bit of a break. You are expected to entertain all of the time. You sing in a world of instant gratification. You do not have the luxury of a long attention span from your listeners. Consequently, you need immediate impact. You must catch the ear and dominate right off the bat.

c) **The technology**

At this point, the classical singing world and the pop singer part company and go very much their separate ways. The classical singer does not use technology. The technology of an opera is 250 plus years old. There are no electronics, no microphones, no electric instruments, no sound engineer, no speakers, no mixing, no pedals, or special effects. Your world is completely different. You play against a background of amplified sound that is electronically modified. Before it even gets to the audience's ears, it has gone through a microphone into an electronic box that produces at the least, amplification and controlled (we hope!) distortion.

It is mixed up with other electronically amplified sounds – at least, drums and guitars, possibly brass and even wind instruments added in – and then it is further processed by a sound engineer and a mixing unit before it is projected in front of the audience. This is not like singing an aria from Tosca. It is a whole different ball game.

So let us ask some very simple questions. You have worked hard in your group, and you have rehearsed and done songs. Then the night of the big show arrives. It is all anticipation and hope. You go on stage, plug in the instruments, fiddle around with amps, microphones and the like. You talk to the sound engineer person(s) at the back of the hall and then you just hope that it all comes out right. When you finally perform, how many of you are able to properly hear your own voice against the music? How many of you have ever taken the trouble to listen to the sound mix at the back of the hall to see what it sounds like? Those of you reading this who are the pros do it and nitpick and get it right. And I bet you have learned a lot you can teach the hopefuls about set up, mix, and balance.

You need a good sound engineer. You need to get the balance right. In a standard pop group, there are usually between three and five electronically amplified instruments on stage, plus one or two voices. The underlying throb is the drum kit. The drum kit is by far the loudest noise on stage. You do not have to amplify drums very much to get one helluva noise. But electronic guitars do need careful handling.

Voice needs even more careful sound engineering. What is the good of singing if you cannot hear your own voice and if, in any event, it is drowned out by over-loud drums and guitars at the back of the theatre, arena, hall, or wherever? The net result is that you find yourself standing on stage with no idea whether you are singing in or out of tune, trying to compete against a cacophony of noise that makes absolutely no sense to you as a singer on stage. So how about trying to get the sound environment right? The pros do not wear cans just to look cool. If you are singing a song, it is the voice that should be at the front of the performance, not the drum kit in the background, which is knocking out 100dbA un-amplified and about 200 dbA when it goes through the sound mixer. Similarly, a good mixer will bring up the lead guitar and bass at the appropriate time. Okay, I know that good sound engineers are hard to find and the kit they use is expensive. But pop and rock music is not exactly a cheap business. The gear is expensive and once you move from that amateur, "in the garage," to doing it, "for real," there is about a 10-fold increase in capital outlay. It is a technologically- driven business. You do need the right gear and the right people to back you up.

General health

In terms of general voice use, the bug bears of pop singers are:

1. over-use

2. dehydration

3. cigarettes or other inhaled substances

4. booze

5. poor posture

6. poor breathing

7. body movements that concentrate on looking cool but prevent good singing technique

8. forcing the voice to try and overcome the sound of electronically amplified instruments

9. pushing the voice for dramatic effect.

By all means look cool, but breathe properly. Do not over-use your voice and do not push your range past that with which you are comfortable. Do not go for added volume and try and compete with amplified instrumentation. That is the sound engineer's job. You should not have to do it. Do remember that no matter how cool you have to look on stage, your posture must be adequate for proper breathing and proper diaphragmatic control of breath outlet. Remember that you need to keep your mouth open and your head up. Do not sing down into your boots. Good tone, good resonance, and good musicality will always be heard by an audience.

Watch the cigarettes and booze. They are not good for your voice. You do not have to be a tee-totaller or stop smoking, just be sensible about what you do in the 48 to 72 hours before a performance. Use good equipment and make sure it is handled properly.

If you are going to get into trouble, it usually manifests itself in one of three ways:

1. Loss of power and/or range. It is the extremes of either or both that will go first.

2. Obvious and audible transition points. At the worst this is vocal break up, with big jumps in range that will become increasingly difficult to control and finally uncontrolled, so that the voice rockets uncontrollably from one range to another. Typical problems are top end and a big gap appears with a quantum leap from normal voice to a strangled falsetto.

3. Throat and neck pain – both of which mean muscle tension – i.e. forcing the voice from the throat and neck.

I hope none of this happens to you. Good singing, and good luck to all. There is a lot of talent out there in terms of voice and instrumental playing and I wish every one of you the best of luck.

Complementary Medicine

Most people think that conventional medicine is their only option. If the doctor cannot cure their ongoing health problem, there is nothing more that can be done.

Complementary medicine, whether naturopathic, or herbal, can solve problems that conventional doctors struggle to even come to terms with.

Conventional doctors often do not know about complementary medicine or nutrition because it is not in their curriculum. Some may have spent some time studying complementary medicine while on the job, but the majority have little knowledge of it.

The basic types of complementary medicine are naturopathic and herbal.

Naturopathy

Merryl Kirkham, Diploma in Naturopathy, Diploma in Clinical Nutrition

Naturopathy embraces drug and chemical-free forms of healing that enable the body to balance and heal itself. If you are experiencing a lack of energy, frequent infections, emotional swings, stress, an upset digestive system, or just generally feeling unwell, naturopathic remedies such as herbs, flower essences, and dietary changes can help you.

We live in a world that is becoming increasingly loaded with toxins, pollutants, and harmful substances. Our foods are often nutrient deficient, devitalised, processed, and contain a wide range of chemicals. We need to ensure our bodies are being well cared for. A healthy lifestyle with daily exercise, adequate sleep, and a balanced diet are all basic requirements for health. Maintain these basics and you are off to a good start.

Vitamins, minerals, proteins, fats, carbohydrates, and water are all essential fuels for our body. Our foods must be chemical-free, unprocessed, and unrefined. To maintain a good level of health, we need to eat a diet rich in organically grown fruits, vegetables, whole grains, and legumes with quality proteins and unsaturated fats. Use sea salt that is unrefined and rich in minerals.

We need to drink at least six glasses of water a day, reduce caffeine and alcohol to a minimum, and remove all drinks containing artificial sugars and chemical additives from our diets. Soft drinks contain lethal chemicals and significantly impact our nervous system. We are surrounded by electrical equipment that gives off electromagnetic radiation, which can cause health problems such as insomnia, anxiety, headaches, and a weakened immune system.

When you are feeling tense, stressed, or worried, remember that your B vitamins are your nerve nutrients. For fears, fright, trauma, or worry, use flower essences such as Rescue Remedy. At times of viral or bacterial infections, you need to support your immune system with extra nutrients and herbs. The most well-known of these are vitamins A, C and E, zinc, selenium, ginger, echinacea, propolis, and garlic (the latter three are also important for throat infections).

To maintain good health, we need to keep a balance between our physical, mental, emotional, and spiritual self. Our bodies have the ability to heal themselves if we listen to them and respond with the right care.

Herbal Medicine

Peter Dunn, R.N. Medical Herbalist. Diploma in Herbal Medicine, Member ATMS

Karen Drummond, R.N. Medical Herbalist. Certified in Aromatherapy, Certified in Therapeutic Massage

Herbal medicine is the oldest form of medicine on our planet and the primary form of medicine for 80 per cent of the world. It incorporates a large body of scientific information and research as well as experience from thousands of years of use. Instead of trying to replace the defensive and restorative systems of the body, as many conventional medicines do, herbal medicine prompts the body to heal itself through the use of herbal supplements.

A typical consultation with a herbalist would include an hour long assessment of a person's diet, lifestyle, and emotional and physical condition in which the patient is viewed holistically. A prescription would then be formulated from a number of herbs (typically four to six) in liquid form. As time goes on and the individual's condition changes, this prescription would be reviewed and adjusted at follow-up consultations.

Another facet of herbal medicine is the use of aromatherapy. Aromatherapy can be used with massage or in other ways, such as inhalation, in the bath or shower, in an oil burner, or on a tissue or spray. It can be used to prevent everyday health problems or as a treatment.

Essential plant oils have a powerful effect on the body and mind. It takes about four seconds for the essential oil to reach the brain through the sense of smell and four minutes to be absorbed into the blood stream through the skin. Stress, antibiotics, inadequate nutrition, and allergies weaken the immune system, which can make us more susceptible to illness. Many essential oils have anti-viral, anti-bacterial, and anti-fungal properties. The throat is the first line of defence and gargling with a few drops of tea tree essential oil in a small glass of water can help destroy many of the germs there and help the lymph glands fight infection. Rubbing diluted essences into the neck glands at the first sign of illness will also help. Sinuses are an important part of voice resonance and allergies such as hay fever, intolerance to house dust, and food allergies can cause sinusitis. Inhaling lavender or a blend of oils such as peppermint, eucalyptus, and tea tree can be very effective.

Massage therapy can also be useful for the mind, body, and emotions as the sense of touch helps release physical and emotional tensions. Massage relaxes and tones muscles, improves circulation in the blood and lymph system, and helps increase the body's immunity to disease. Muscles receive an increased blood supply of nutrients that help to improve functioning. Massage can relieve chronic neck and shoulder tension, which can cause back pain and headaches. Aromatherapy massage utilises the power of essential plant oils for specific effects on the body and mind. Trigger point therapy works on taut fibrous bands in the muscle tissue, which can feel like a knot and can cause pain when stimulated. Regular massage is cumulative for health and also provides a time for quiet contemplation and peace in a busy world.

Long-Term Health Choices for Singers

There are many choices to make during the course of your life and it is not my place to tell you which ones are the right ones. What you will find in this short section are a few facts and suggestions with regard to body piercing and dental treatment. All I can do is to urge you to take this information on board.

Body piercing

Body piercing and studs are made from a collection of heavy metals that can be dangerous to your health. The metals may be copper, lead, nickel or silver – some even contain mercury. Heavy metals such as these are not compatible with our body chemistries and can cause poisoning in the long-term. Each day a stud comes into contact with saliva or other body fluids, it carries poisonous metals throughout the delicate body tissues. The body tries to ward off infection and our immune system tries to protect us, but chronic diseases can often eventuate over time. Symptoms as minor as constant colds or flu, sore throats, headaches, or migraines may be covering up much more serious problems. For a singer, these problems may cut short a flourishing career or have detrimental effects for the future.

The single most important concern for singers is the throat or larynx area and the thyroid gland. As time goes by, the heavy metals will affect the sound quality of the voice and one's health in general. Heavy metals are known as stealth killers because they can take years or even decades to manifest themselves in the body. They can reap a whole heap of havoc ranging from immune system disorders, depression, dry eyes and tinnitus (ringing in the ears), to asthma, bronchitis, migraines, and croup.

Tattoos

Tattoos, although fashionable, are best avoided. They poison your immune system long-term and can lead to serious health and wellness challenges as you age.

Amalgam fillings

Amalgam dental fillings and root canals can also be dangerous if your dentist is using the wrong materials. If possible, find yourself a, 'no mercury,' dentist who applies the latest protocols commenced by Professor Hal Huggins. You should ask to be given toxin-free alternatives such as biologically compatible fillings that can be tested for your body's chemistry. For example, the Voco range of dental composites and bonding materials can be put in fillings. Or contact Dental Amalgam Mercury Support (DAMS) for a listing of dentists who are aware of the damage mercury and other non-compatible fillings can do. The New Zealand group is called DAMS NZ Incorporated.

If you want to find out more about dental and digestive health, the following books are invaluable:

Essential Oils Integrative Medical Guide, D. Gary Young, N.D.

It's All in Your Head, Professor Hal Huggins PhD, DDS, M.S.

Uninformed Consent, Hal A Huggins and Thomas E Levy M.D. J.D.

Digestive Wellness, Elizabeth Lipski, PhD CCN.

The Healing Power of 8 Sugars, Allan C Somersall, PhD, M.D.

The Eat Right Diet, Dr Peter D'Adamo and Catherine Whitney.

Cosmetics Unmasked, Dr Stephen Antczak and Gina Antczak.

Your Health at Risk, Dr Toni Jeffries, PhD.

The Cure for all Diseases, Hulda Regehr Clark, PhD, N.D.

How to Survive on a Toxic Planet, Dr Steve Nugent, CCN.

How to Cure and Prevent any Disease, Ray Gebauer, preventative medicine specialist.

I Can Sing, But Where is My Voice?

Scales and Sounds to Practice

Practice the following scales and sounds daily to improve your vocal range and the quality of your voice.

To start with spend 15 minutes daily to warm up. Practice down the scale. A — E — I — O — U. Work through your three octaves gently and be patient with yourself as you develop your range of 37 notes.

Scale sounds

ah ba fa ca pa ma da ra

oo oo oo oo oo oo oo oo

Lip notes: bae be bi bo boo
                  lae lee li loo loo
                  mae me mi mo moo

forty fae (two "a" sounds on fae silent "e")

pay pay pay pay pay pay pay

nae nae nae nae nae nae nae

ee ee ee ee ee ee ee

For breaking phlegm: cookoo cookoo coo caw caw caw (repeat for three minutes)

Rounded lips: loo loo loo loo loo

cookoo cookoo coo oo oh ah (pronounced as AR)

Sounds

Practice the following sounds to semi-tones and tones. Make sure you do this in front of a mirror to ensure the correct position of the jaw, mouth, and tongue is used.

oo oo oo oo oo oo oo oo

bae be bi bo boo

lae lee li lo loo

mae me mi mo moo

oh no woe

oh ah ee

hmm hmm

loo loo loo

coo kick kah kah

forty fae

mo me mini moo

evermore

cookoo cookoo coo caw caw caw

cookoo cookoo coo oo oh ah

up pup, up pup, up pup, up pup
(do this slowly at first, then gradually faster)

me me me, me me me, me me me
(do this fast, in lots of three)

pay tay

ah ba fa ca pa ma ra da

ba-i-ley say-ay re-oh

ming mong ming moo

hi bubare bub bub

do re me fa so la ti do, do re me fa so la ti do

coo kick kah kah

rolo polo

I Can Sing, But Where is My Voice?

in bo boo, tim bo boo

I sky, high sky, I cry, I can cry, I fly

tra ra

ga-ay roses

ding dong ding dong doo

bring bong bing boo

lae lee li lo loo

swing wing thing

timbo bo boo in bo boo

hi ho hini hoo

Billy Boggs blew back the blackboard.

Did Billy Boggs blow back the blackboard?

If Billy Boggs blew back the blackboard,

where is the blackboard Billy Boggs blew back?

Peter Piper picked a peck of pickled peppers.

But the peck of pickled peppers that Peter Piper picked were poor.

So Peter Piper picked another peck of pickled peppers and threw away the peck of pickled peppers that were poor.

Worksheets

1) Here are some enjoyable vocal exercises, handed down over the years from teacher to student. Male voices, sing these an octave lower.

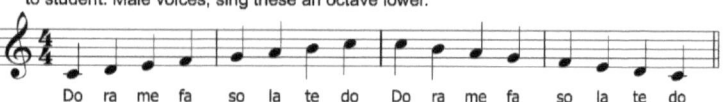

2) The following should be practiced in several different keys. Take it up or down in tones or semitones to gradually increase your range. Remember to apply the correct resonance.

Remember that the second "k" in this exercise should come with an audible breath.

3) Remember the mouth position for "e" and "o". Practice in front of a mirror to check lip, mouth and head position.

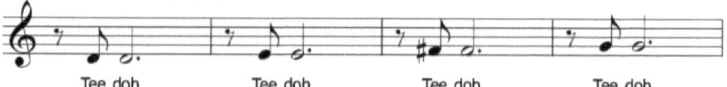

4) This exercise requires the correct mouth positions for "o", "ee" (ty) and "a", ending with a short "e" after the "a". Do this exercise in one breath.

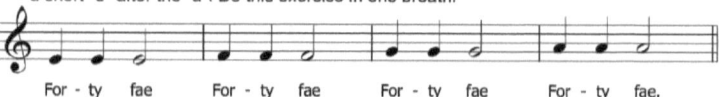

5) Smile for the "in" and "im" sound, - this is a very quick lip movement.

6) In this exercise remember to roll the "r" and place the mouth in the correct position for the "o" sound. Do this in one breath.

7) This exercise is a play on the "i" sound. Drop the jaw three finger width. Finish the sound, then close the mouth.

8) Remember the basic mouth position for "a" and keep this shape throughout the exercise. Listen for clarity of sound.

I Can Sing, But Where is My Voice?

9) Sing this exercise for ten minutes up and down semitones. This will clear a nasal drip!

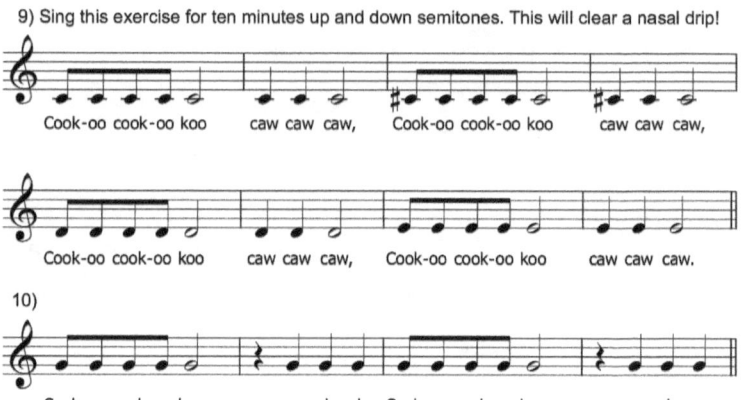

10)

11) Apply the basic position of the mouth for the "a" sound and roll the "r".

12) Blow out the first "p" sound on the word 'up' keeping it light. Do the same for the second and third "p"s on pup.

13) Apply the basic position of the mouth for the "a" sound remembering to open the mouth separately for each new sound.

14) Make the lips work hard for this exercise. Start with tones then try semitones.

15) Use the basic "e", "o" and "u" lip positions for this exercise.

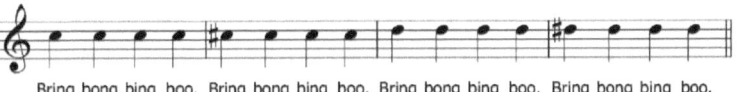

Bring bong bing boo, Bring bong bing boo, Bring bong bing boo, Bring bong bing boo.

16) In one breath, try these two exercises with the single vowel sounds, - "A, E, I, O, U". Make one vowel sound only, not two or three.

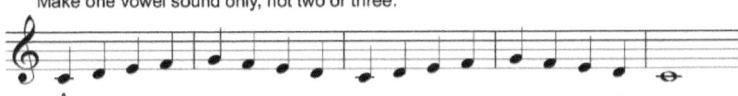

A - - - - - - - - - - - - - - -

A - - - - - - - - - - - - - - -

17) Pitch practice. Listen and learn to identify and repeat each pitch/tone of the four "Cs" giving you your three octave range.

18) Try the basic "a" sound here.

La la la la la la la la la la la la la la la la

19) Working with the "a" sound taking care to avoid breath before tone, (i.e. making two sounds).

Bai - ley sai - rey oh   Bai - ley sai - rey oh   Bai - ley sai - rey oh

20) Ensure the muscles of the mouth work hard by 'smiling' the "e" sounds.

We be see free,   We be see free,   We be see free,   We be see free.

Answers To Question Time

(page 63)

1. Mouth

2. No

3. Diaphragm

4. You use your quadratus lumborum (lower centre back), latissimus dorsi (sides of back), intercostal (support diaphgram), diaphragmatic (diaphragm), sterno-thyroid (throat and neck) and cleido-mastoid (chewing) muscles.

5. Use a level flat surface such as a stool to sit on and ensure that your knees are lower than your pelvis.

6. No

7. No. Stillness and ease of movement is the best policy.

8. A good place to look is to a point on foreheads, just above the eyes, which makes an audience think you are looking into their eyes.

9. Using high resonance, place the sound on the hard

palate (roof of your mouth). It will resound and sound full and fat.

10. Always in through the mouth, to and from the diaphragm.

11. Practice deep breathing exercises until you can blow out for 90 to 120 seconds.

12. You can achieve good diction if you over-accentuate the use of the lips which are the "speaker cones" of the body carrying the sound you make to the back of the room.

13. Yes, gently on words that start with a vowel sound when necessary, to give clarity.

14. Use a Shure SM58 microphone, or similar, to sing through. This type of microphone is cylindrical in pick up. So place your thumb under the rim at the bottom of the head and relax your fingers around the stem of the microphone. Make sure it is a relaxed grip, not tight. Hold the microphone just under your lips. Aim for the centre at the top of your lips. Hold it around 10 centimetres away from your mouth. The audience needs to see your mouth as you sing. Practice in the mirror until you manage this.

15. Place the sound on the roof of your mouth (hard palate).

16. Using expelled air correctly to sing high or low notes.

17. Feet shoulder width apart. Knees unlocked (not bent). Weight slightly on the balls of your feet, slightly to the outside. Make sure your head is level (not to the side). Chin tucked in slightly. When positioned correctly, the chin sits just above the second button level of a shirt. Girls need to be aware that high heels do not help position the muscles which support your larynx in a good place. This can make your sound weak and thin.

18. Practice gently and daily for at least six weeks with one day off a week. The night before a performance get a full night's uninterrupted sleep. Drink water at regular intervals and eat a well-balanced meal. The hour before going on stage do your warm-ups, deep breathing, scales for 15 minutes and run through the song.

19. No. You should not sing when you have a cold or a flu. If you do, you risk severe damage to the delicate tissues of the vocal muscles by working them when they are infected. Instead rest until your speaking voice is back to normal.

20. Yes with due diligence and regular input. Also, being prepared to hear singing that is terrible at first but keep on going and relax. Repetition delivers results in the end.

21. Always begin with deep breathing, scales and exercises. An hour or two goes by very quickly and does prepare you for what lies ahead in the songs you need to tackle. Remember gentle practice, not loud forceful practice, is best as it gradually strengthens the vocal muscles.

22. If you cannot read music, you can feel it through desire, intent and lots of practice. But it is good to have a little knowledge of the theory of music, and if all fails start by applying the answer to question 23.

23. Knowing your scales and exercises and how to sing in tune and in time.

24. Gradual, regular practice over a long period of time. For 12 months or more practice scales and diction.

25. Yes. Always practice your scales at the beginning of practice sessions, before your songs.

26. Yes. Cigarettes are loaded with toxic chemicals that can deeply affect your immune system, destroying the delicate mucus membranes of your throat. Smoking can cause long-term health issues with a lot of unnecessary suffering and numerous visits to the doctor. Also, have a thought for those around you who do not smoke. Your breath is not nice and your clothes reek.

27. Yes.

28. Daily practice of singing long, smooth notes. Hold notes for up to 16 bars. You can daydream while doing this as the time passes really quickly when you are relaxed.

29. Practice breathing for singing daily (in and out through your mouth) gradually lengthening the time you breathe out. Adults: 120 seconds. Children 45 seconds.

You need to have fully developed your breathing and resonances both high and low.

30. Singing all your notes from the throat where notes are not made.

31. By practicing deep breathing all your career and not smoking.

32. If you can hear accurately, and are not physically deaf, you can learn to hear and repeat sounds accurately by learning scales.

33. Slurring and scooping is singing one or more notes before the note that is required. A glottal attack on vowel sounds will resolve this. Know your scales in tones and semi-tones and avoid running words together.

34. Place, rather than force, high resonance notes.

35. You need to know where you are singing at any given time. Most singers will have a two or three octave range. Differentiate between low, mid and high toned octaves. Master this and you will survive long term.

36. So people can hear and understand what you are singing.

37. Ensure there is a monitor speaker placed a metre or so away at your feet in front of you. Cup your hand to your ear. Ensure you have a Shure SM58 or similar

vocal microphone. It has the best pick-up surround sound. There will be later models nowadays but for public performance the SM58 has been tried and faithful for over 40 years and used by all the big stars.

38. No. Train your tongue to lie flat and relax.

39. No. Sing intelligently using the skills you began with.

40. If you have done your deep breathing all along and you apply this before singing, you are focused to give your best.

Career and Photo Gallery

On the next few pages are highlights of my 47 years in show business. I have included some references given along the way from those who enjoyed my work and put pen to paper. You will note there have been many spellings of my name such as Ricci, Rikki or Ricki. It seems no two people spell the same way.

Fifth form fun at basketball camp, Hamilton, New Zealand (Ricci with guitar)

Passed exams 1965, with proud mum Una at Waikato Hospital

Sydney, first professional photos for Leagues/RSL circuit

Maori Miners, Terrigal NSW, 1967

I Can Sing, But Where is My Voice?

Maori Miners, Terrigal NSW, 1967

Publicity photos for Chicago University Campus, Da Nang Beach, Vietnam, 1968

Swinging 7 Revue ex Sydney, Tuy Hoa Airmen's NCO, US Forces, Vietnam

With Donnie James Show, 1968, US Forces Tours

Pleiku, Vietnam, 1968

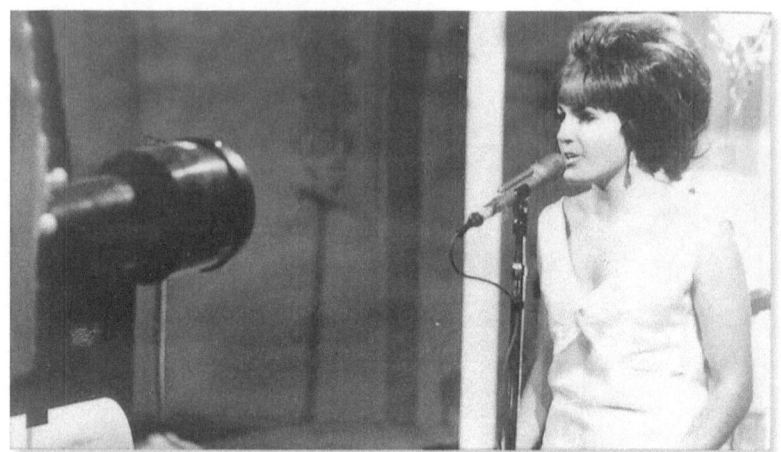

US Armed Forces Vietnam Television Network (AFVNTV) Nashville Vietnam Television Show, regular singer, 1968

Publicity photo for concert tour, NSW

On tour in the Philippines with the Reycards, Tropical Palace, Manila, 1977

NSW Club Circuit, 1973

Extra for Rush, ABC TV

Kenny Johnston's Big Band, Newtown Leagues Club, Sydney, 1972

Rnr in Hawaii, 1978

Publicity photos for my own cabaret shows throughout New Zealand, 1984

I Can Sing, But Where is My Voice?

Williams Road and Waterfront, P.O. Box 40, Paihia, New Zealand.
Telephones 27-099, 27-036, 27-811. Telex NZ 21616.

11 January 1982

TO WHOM IT MAY CONCERN:

RICCI CARR'S CAPE BRETT CONCERT

This is to confirm that Ricci Carr was employed aboard our cruise vessel, "Tiger Lily II" from 30 November 1981 to 11 January 1982.

Ricci was entertaining daily on our 4:00p.m./7:00p.m. Cape Brett cruise and was also the cruise director.

Apart from being a polished and professional entertainer, we found Ricci helpful with all aspects of the cruise and in particular she was extremely capable in dealing with our passengers needs.

In itself the Ricci Carr Cape Brett Concert was extremely successful, this result in no small way was due to Ricci's excellent musical ability and versatility.

We highly recommend Ricci Carr.

Yours faithfully,
MOUNT COOK LINE

JOHN KANE
Regional Manager

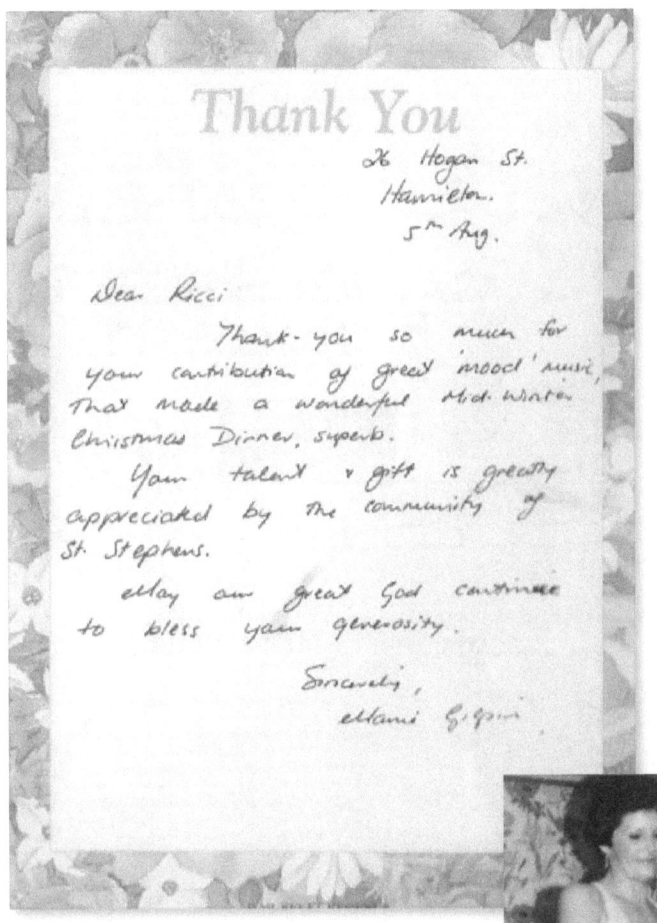

Cabaret in the Bay of Islands

I Can Sing, But Where is My Voice?

Ricci Carr's
CAPE BRETT CONCERT

ABOARD TIGER LILY

DEPARTS: 4.00 p.m.   RETURNS: 7.00 p.m.
30th DECEMBER THRU 10TH JANUARY

Not only will you cruise to Cape Brett and the famous Hole in the Rock but you will also experience the music that has made Ricci Carr on of New Zealands most sought after entertainers.

The perfect way to relax after that hard day on the beach.

ALL PASSENGERS ON THE RICCI CARR CRUISE ARE IN TO WIN!!!

 WIN A 7 DAY HOLIDAY ON BEAUTIFUL TREASURE ISLAND FLYING AIRPACIFIC

> Melanie & Philip Blackburne
> 109 Portland Road
> Remuera
> AUCKLAND 5
>
> Dear Ricki –
>
> We're *so* pleased you didn't have to go off to Auckland at an early hour, & could stay & enjoy yourself for the evening.
>
> The solo was just perfect – incredibly moving, just what we wanted! And the rest of music was wonderful – everybody enjoyed it & many have commented so favourably.
>
> Good luck with all of your plans – I don't know how you cope with all the changes that take place!
> Take care – Regards
> Melanie & Philip.

Cocktail hour, easy listening music on grand piano with vocals, Hyatt Hotel, Auckland

Duo with Gavin Hawley, Hamilton pub scene, 1986

I Can Sing, But Where is My Voice?

To Whom it may concern

This is to certify that Miss Rikki Carr was employed by Club Mirage for the past eight months.

Miss Carr was employed as a pianist/vocalist to entertain our guests during the first two and a half hours of dinner. She was very much appreciated and many favourable comments were passed about her. Miss Carr was always reliable, well groomed and conducted herself in a professional manner.

We would reccommend her most highly for any position she may wish to apply for in this field.

Emerald Alba

Emerald Alba

Proprietor.
30th October, 1980.

CLUB MIRAGE

Freybery Place, 33 High St. P.O. Box 3370, Auckland, New Zealand. Telephone: 31 904 or 31 336

Travelodge Auckland

96-100 Quay St, Auckland 1.
P.O. Box 459, Auckland, New Zealand.
Telephone 770-349
Telex: N.Z. 2538

31 August 1981

TO WHOM IT MAY CONCERN

This letter serves to confirm that Ricki Carr was contracted by Auckland Travelodge from 10 October 1980 to 26 September 1981.

Ricki entertained in "Barnaby's" restaurant on Friday and Saturday nights from 7.30 pm to 11.30 pm.

During her time with us Ricki provided a high standard of entertainment and at all times behaved in an extremely professional manner. Her contract has not been renewed as a result of changes in our entertainment programme but I would have no hesitation in endorsing her already established reputation as a thoroughly competent and professional entertainer.

P A HOBBS
General Manager

I Can Sing, But Where is My Voice?

HOTEL INTER·CONTINENTAL AUCKLAND

EXECUTIVE OFFICE

13th March 1981

TO WHOM IT MAY CONCERN

This is to certify that Rikki Carr has been employed by this Hotel for approximately one year as a Pianist/Key-Boards player and as a Singer in our Top Of The Town Restaurant and Functions Rooms.

During the time Rikki has been performing for us we have always found her to be very popular with our guests and an extremely talented lady.

I have no hesitation in recommending Rikki to any future employer.

Yours faithfully

J.P. Vowles
MANAGER

PRINCES STREET, AUCKLAND, NEW ZEALAND   TELEPHONE: 797-220 BOX 3938 CABLE: INHOTELCOR
(A VACATION GROUP HOTEL)

benny levin promotions ltd

13th April 1992

TO WHOM IT MAY CONCERN

I am delighted to give this recommendation to one of New Zealand's top singer/songwriters, Ricci Carr. She is an extremely talented lady and her original material for her forthcoming album is quite stunning.

Ricci Carr is a proven professional entertainer and deserves to be recognised for her outstanding talent.

Yours faithfully,

B.J. Levin
MANAGING DIRECTOR

P.O. Box 5564 Auckland, New Zealand Ph: (09) 797-784. Fax: (09) 3098-342

Solo grand piano, New Year's Eve Concert, Rotorua Convention Centre, 1994

Guest vocalist with Ian Metcalfe's Cranston Catering, "Affirmation", John Worth's Band, Rose Gardens, Hamilton, Christmas 1990

With my recording crew for the album Moonlight Reflections for NZBC National Radio Concerts, 1990/91

Recording Moonlight Reflections

National Radio

Wellington NZ
Broadcasting House,
Bowen Street
PO Box 2396
Telephone (04) 474-1999
Fax (04) 474-1454

LETTER OF INTRODUCTION

TO WHOM IT MAY CONCERN

This serves to introduce singer/songwriter Ricci Carr from Rotorua, New Zealand.

As producers of her material, we highly recommend that you listen to this artist's tape with the view to offering her a release deal in your country.

Should you require any further information or wish to negotiate a potential licensing contract, please contact the writer.

Dick Le Fort
Executive Music Producer

24 July 1992

A Network Service of
Radio New Zealand Ltd

With Liam Ryan (The Narcs) mixing own original tracks for Lifetimes CD album, Auckland, New Zealand. 1986

Completion of solo grand piano contract at Hyatt Hotel, Auckland

Acknowledgements

There are many people to thank for their willingness to help in the publication process. Without them, all this would not have come to pass.

Thanks to

Bridget May-Levis for her drawings.

Michelle May for initial proof reading, and encouragement to continue in all kinds of weather over the years.

Gavin Hawley at Moonglow Music for worksheets.

James Heffield and Samuel Hemrom, my initial project editors.

Initially, David Chen for formatting this work of art.

Peter Blake, Otolaryngologist and head and neck surgeon for his wise words.

Peter Dunn, Botannicals Herbal Dispensary

Meryl Kirkham, N.D. Massage

Thanks to my very special students who shared their experiences

Savannah, Ben, JF, Teri, Sandey, Leonie, Keith, Mary-Sue, Mareta, Helen, Rebecca, Leo, Jim, Andrew, Shelley, Jess, Benjamin, Fiona and to my many students who teach me every day.

The *I can sing, but where is my voice?* eBook and easy listening music *Lifetimes* album can be uploaded from online book and music stores or from www.icansing.co

Original easy listening songs by Ricci Carr.
Available at: www.icansing.co

www.ingramcontent.com/pod-product-compliance
Lightning Source LLC
Chambersburg PA
CBHW031422290426
44110CB00011B/488